A Student's Guide to INDONESIAN Grammar

Dwi Noverini Djenar

OXFORD
UNIVERSITY PRESS
AUSTRALIA & NEW ZEALAND

OXFORD
UNIVERSITY PRESS

253 Normanby Road, South Melbourne, Victoria 3205, Australia

Oxford University Press is a department of the University of Oxford. It furthers the University's objective of excellence in research, scholarship, and education by publishing worldwide in

Oxford New York

Auckland Cape Town Dar es Salaam Hong Kong Karachi Kuala Lumpur Madrid Melbourne Mexico City Nairobi New Delhi Shanghai Taipei Toronto

With offices in

Argentina Austria Brazil Chile Czech Republic France Greece Guatemala Hungary Italy Japan Poland Portugal Singapore South Korea Switzerland Thailand Turkey Ukraine Vietnam

OXFORD is a trade mark of Oxford University Press in the UK and in certain other countries

First published 2003
Reprinted 2005, 2009, 2011

National Library of Australia

Cataloguing-in-Publication data:

Djenar, Dwi Noverini, 1961-

A student's guide to Indonesian grammar.
Includes index.
For secondary students in years 10–12 and beginning tertiary students.

ISBN 978 0 19 551466 7.

1. Indonesian language—Textbooks for foreign speakers—English I Title.
499.22182421

Typeset by Sylvia Witte
Printed in Hong Kong by Sheck Wah Tong Printing Press Ltd.

Contents

Introduction

A Student's Guide to Indonesian Grammar is intended for secondary students in Years 10–12 and for tertiary students beginning Indonesian. It presents grammar in an accessible and fun way by focusing on its use in daily communication. Many of the exercises in this book are designed for pair or group interaction, while others are suitable for independent learning.

The earlier chapters in the book cover lighter topics, such as asking and answering questions, numbers and prepositions. Subsequent chapters cover more difficult topics. Teachers may wish to use the easier chapters in the early part of the year as a warm-up, if their students have already studied the topics beforehand, then move on to other chapters. Each chapter is self-contained, allowing teachers to select topics to coincide with other teaching materials. Cross-referencing within and between chapters provides easy access to related grammatical points.

Each chapter in this book covers one grammatical topic. For each part of the topic, an explanation is given, supported by examples. Exercises (**Latihan**) provide immediate reinforcement of the grammar learnt. Vocabulary (**Kosakata**) is given for many of the exercises. Where a dictionary may be required, this is clearly specified.

Grammar is an integral part of language use. It forms part of how people communicate with each other in daily life. Often a communicative situation determines people's choice of words and way of saying things. For example, people may speak differently in informal and formal situations. In addition, people may write differently from the way they speak. The communicative dimensions are complex and are impossible to be dealt with comprehensively in a book of this sort. However, throughout this book, in the explanations of grammatical topics and in the accompanying exercises, indications are provided as to the situations in which certain language uses are most appropriate.

Additional information is given under the following headings.

- **Did you know?**
- **Note**
- **Handy expression**
- **Be careful!**

This information relates to useful expressions, cultural notes and errors to avoid, which students and teachers may find interesting and helpful.

The introduction of grammatical terms is unavoidable in a grammar book and some learners may find this rather daunting. In this book, grammatical terms are used only where no simpler alternative is available. Grammatical terms introduced for the first time are italicised and an explanation of the term is provided.

Acknowledgments

The suggestion for this book was first put to me by Ray O'Farrell, the publishing director at Oxford University Press, when my son Haris was merely three months old. A year later, I began to work on the manuscript. Ray has since moved to another position and so has not seen this work in its completed form, but I am very grateful to him for initiating the project in the first place. Lisa Carroll, my publisher, has followed this project through. Many thanks also go to her.

This book has benefited greatly from comments and criticisms from many people. I would especially like to thank Linda Hibbs, Paul Fyffe, Nyoman Riasa and an anonymous reviewer, who all made detailed comments on the manuscript. My students at La Trobe University trialed the chapters and questioned a number of points. I much appreciate their useful suggestions. My thanks also go to those who furnished examples or made suggestions through various discussions on Indonesian grammar, particularly Umar Muslim, Harry Aveling, and Peter Chamberlain. Ron Baird and Tracy Lee in the Department of Asian Studies at La Trobe University provided much needed technical assistance. I thank them both for their help. This book owes a great deal of its present form to my editors, Stephen Roche and Jenny Bilos. I am very grateful to both of them for their hard work.

Some of the ideas in this book have been inspired by other works on grammar, in particular *An A–Z of English Grammar & Usage* by Geoffrey Leech (Longman, 1989), *Grammar Practice Activities* by Penny Ur (Cambridge University Press, 1988), and *Indonesian Reference Grammar* by James Sneddon (Allen & Unwin, 1996).

This book is for Haris, from whose mouth springs forth ever so effortlessly one object-focus sentence after another.

Source Acknowledgments

The author and publisher wish to thank copyright holders for granting permission to reproduce copyright materials. Copyright holders are acknowledged where known, otherwise sources are indicated.

The Adventures of TINTIN by Hergè © Moulinsart SA, Belgium: pp. 104 (top), 168, 169 and 181. Descriptions and photos of Kemiri and Pala dan Bunga Pala sourced from *Masakan Indonesia*, PT Gramedia Pustaka Utama, Jakarta, 1997: p. 133. Sumpah Pemuda (Youth Pledge), Youth Conference, 28 October 1928: p. 67. Song lyrics from *Jika* written by Melly Goeslaw and Ari Lasso: p. 148. 'Fisika itu Asyik' advertisement, *Kompas*, Jakarta, 13 February 2000: p. 186.

Every effort has been made to trace the original source of all material reproduced in this book. Where the attempt has been unsuccessful, the author and publisher would be pleased to hear from the copyright holder concerned to rectify the omission.

1 Asking and Answering Questions

1.1 Asking questions

There are different ways of asking questions in Indonesian, as in English. Sentences that ask questions are called *interrogative* sentences. In this chapter we look at ways of asking and answering questions.

Raised intonation

One simple way of asking questions in Indonesian is by raising our intonation. In writing, this is indicated by a question mark. Except for this question mark, the sentence looks exactly the same as a statement.

Kamu mahasiswa?
Are you a university student? (Literally: You are a university student?)

Anda tinggal di sini?
Do you live here? (Literally: You live here?)

Dia sakit?
Is he/she sick? (Literally: He/she is sick?)

Using *apa(kah)*

Another way of asking questions is by using **apakah** at the beginning of a sentence. The word **apakah**, like the word 'do' in English when you ask 'Do you live here?', does not have a meaning in itself; it simply tells us that the sentence is a question. **Apakah** makes the question sound formal.

Apakah anda tinggal di sini?
Do you live here?

Apakah dia suka apel?
Does he/she like apples?

You can make the questions less formal by dropping the **-kah** at the end of this question word.

Apa anda tinggal di sini?
Apa dia suka apel?

Note

Apa also means 'what'. You will know which one is intended by remembering this: **apa** as a question word (short for **apakah**) is placed at the beginning of the sentence, whereas **apa** (what) can also be placed at the end.

Question word:

> **Apa itu apel?**
> Is that an apple?

'What':

> **Apa nama apel itu?**
> What is the name of that apple?
>
> **Nama apel itu apa?**
> What is the name of that apple?

LATIHAN 1

Ask a question in Indonesian about each of the following pictures using raised intonation, **apa(kah)** or **apa**.

KOSAKATA

ape	apple
burung	bird
es krim	icecream
jeruk	orange
keju	cheese
kue ulang tahun	birthday cake
nanas	pineapple
nasi	cooked rice
pisang	banana
susu	milk

Example:

Apa(kah) ini apel? Ini apa?

Questions with 'wh-' words

Some questions are referred to in English as 'wh-' questions because most of the question words start with 'wh-'; for example, 'what', 'who', 'where' and 'when'. The Indonesian equivalents of these question words are discussed below.

APA: 'WHAT'

Apa is used to ask about objects, concrete or abstract. It means 'what' or 'what kind of'.

Apa nama binatang itu?
What is the name of that animal?

Musik apa itu?
What kind of music is that?

Nama sekolah itu apa?
What is the name of that school? (Literally: The name of that school is what?)

SIAPA: 'WHO'

Siapa is used to ask questions to do with a person, such as a person's name, who a person is, or to whom an object belongs.

Siapa dia?
Who is he/she?

Siapa namanya?
What is his/her name?

Tas siapa ini?
Whose bag is this?
(The bag is associated with the person who owns it.)

Be careful!
In English we use 'what' when asking names (for example, 'What is your name?'). Indonesian speakers think of the person when asking the same question, so they use **siapa**, not **apa**. If you use **apa**, it sounds like you are asking about an object rather than a person.

BERAPA: 'HOW MANY', 'HOW MUCH'

Berapa is used to ask questions to do with numbers and quantity, such as the number of people, weight and measurements.

Berapa orang datang ke pesta itu?
How many people came to that party?

Halaman berapa?
What page? (In Indonesian the question literally means 'Page how many?'. **Berapa** is used because the answer has to do with numbers.)

You can also add **ke** to this question word to mean 'what number' in a numerical series.

A: **Kamu anak keberapa?**
Which child are you? (Literally: What number child are you?)

B: **Saya anak ke dua.**
I am the secondchild.

MANA

Mana is used in questions, usually not by itself, but attached to the preposition **di**, **ke** or **dari**: **di mana** (where), **ke mana** (where to), **dari mana** (where from). These expressions can be placed either at the beginning or at the end of a sentence.

> **Di mana kamu tinggal?**
> Where do you live?
>
> **Mereka pergi ke mana?**
> Where are they going?/Where did they go?
>
> **Dari mana uang ini?**
> Where is this money from? (Where did you get it from?)

Mana can also be preceded by the word **yang** to ask 'which one'.

> **Yang mana mobilmu?**
> Which one is your car?
>
> **Topimu yang mana?**
> Which one is your hat?

KAPAN: 'WHEN'

Kapan is used to ask about a particular point in time or duration.

> **Kapan liburan sekolah mulai?**
> When does the school holiday start?
>
> **Kapan anda akan datang?**
> When are you coming?

Even though **kapan** translates into English as 'when', it is only used in questions. We cannot use it as a *conjunction* (to connect one part of a sentence with another), as in 'I was watching television when she arrived' or 'When I was born, my mother was 33'. For expressions like these, we use **ketika** or **waktu**.

MENGAPA, KENAPA: 'WHY'

Mengapa and **kenapa** both mean 'why'. However, **kenapa** is more informal.

> **Mengapa anda terlambat?**
> Why are you late?
>
> **Kenapa kamu diam saja?**
> Why are you quiet (not saying anything)?

BAGAIMANA: 'HOW'

Bagaimana is used in different situations, from a simple everyday question, such as 'how are you', to ways of doing something.

> **Bagaimana kabarmu? (= Apa kabar?)**
> How are you?
>
> **Bagaimana caranya mengupas kelapa?**
> How do we open (literally 'peel') a coconut?

LATIHAN 2

Ask a question in Indonesian about each of these pictures using specific question words ('wh-' question words).

1 Who is she?

2 What page, Miss?

3 How are you?

4 Why is he crying?

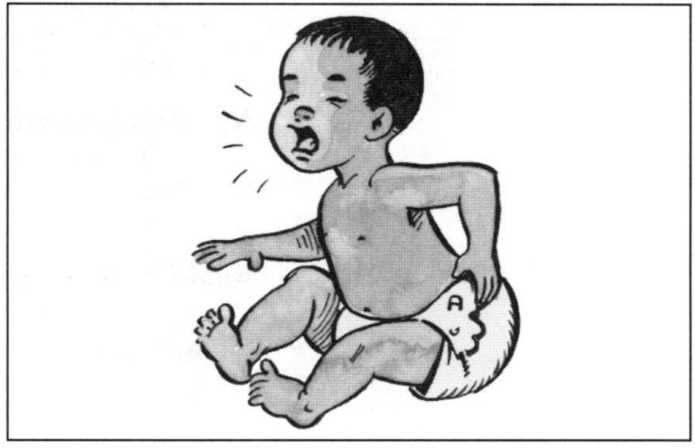

Using tags *bukan* and *ya*

Another form of question is with tags, such as **bukan** and **ya**. This type of question is more like seeking confirmation from the person to whom you are talking. **Bukan** is formal and is therefore not suitable to use with friends. Its short version, **kan**, is more informal and is equivalent to **ya** when used in questions. Both tags are widely used in spoken Indonesian.

Anda guru, <u>bukan</u>?
You are a teacher, aren't you?

Saudara setuju dengan kami, <u>bukan</u>?
You agree with us, don't you?

Kamu tinggal di rumah itu <u>kan</u>?
You live in that house, don't you?

Kalian bergurau <u>kan</u>?
You are all joking, aren't you?

Ini kelas bahasa Indonesia <u>ya</u>?
This is Indonesian class, isn't it?

Jill orang Australia <u>ya</u>?
Jill is an Australian, isn't she?

1.2 Giving answers

Just as there are different ways of asking questions, there are different ways of responding to them. Some common ways of answering questions are discussed below.

Positive answers with *ya* or *iya*

To give a positive answer in Indonesian, we can use the word **ya**.

A: **Anda wartawan?**
Are you a journalist?
B: **<u>Ya</u>.**
Yes.

Often people say **iya** to emphasise or confirm an answer. **Iya** can be used, for example, to respond to tag questions.

A: **Kamu kakak Susan kan?**
You are Susan's older sibling, aren't you?
B: **<u>Iya</u>.**
Yes.

Anak: **Pak, nanti liburan sekolah kita ke Jakarta ya?**
Dad, next school holiday we're going to Jakarta, aren't we?
Bapak: **<u>Iya</u>.**
Yes, all right.

LATIHAN 3

Ask questions using the tags **bukan**, **kan** or **ya**. Remember that these tags differ in their degree of formality. Use them appropriately by taking into account the person to whom you are talking. Answer each question using **ya** or **iya**.

1. To a stranger at a bank: 'Today is 15 June, isn't it?'
2. To your mother: 'This chicken is for me, isn't it?'
3. To your older sister: 'You like that film, don't you?'

4 To your teacher: 'Our homework is page 12, isn't it?'
5 To a bus driver: 'This bus goes to the shopping centre, doesn't it?' ('Go to' = **ke**. You do not need to translate 'go', because **ke** + place-name already means 'go'; for example, **ke toko** means 'go to the shop'.)

Negative answers with *tidak, bukan or belum*

To give a negative answer in Indonesian, we need to choose between three words: **tidak**, **bukan** or **belum**.

BUKAN

Bukan is used to negate a noun (that is, when you want to negate a thing, whether concrete, such as a book, or abstract, such as a name). In the examples below, the negated words are underlined.

A: **Ini bukumu?**
Is this your book?
B: **Bukan.**
No, it's not.

A: **Nama anda Raymond?**
Is your name Raymond?
B: **Bukan.**
No, it's not.

TIDAK

Tidak is used to negate everything else other than a noun (verbs, adjectives, adverbs).

A: **Bapakmu bekerja di kantor itu?**
Does your father work in that office?
B: **Tidak.**
No, he doesn't.

A: **Apakah anda suka film horor?**
Do you like horror films?
B: **Tidak.**
No, I don't.

BELUM

Belum means 'not yet' and is used to indicate that something is not yet done.

Leni: **Nia, kamu sudah makan?**
Nia, have you eaten?
Nia: **Belum.**
No, not yet.

Belum can also be used to answer the 'Have you ever ...?' type of question.

A: **Apakah anda pernah ke Indonesia?**
Have you ever been to Indonesia?
B: **Belum.**
No, I haven't. (No, not yet.)

A: **Kamu pernah makan durian?**
Have you ever eaten a durian?
B: **Belum.**
No, I haven't. (No, not yet.)

LATIHAN 4

The following game, called **Siapa saya?**, is an exercise in asking questions with raised intonation and **apa(kah)**, and giving positive answers with **ya** and negative answers with **tidak** or **bukan**.

Procedure:
One person in the class is chosen to assume the identity of a certain character (person, cartoon character or an animal). The character is chosen by the rest of the class without the person knowing. (Ask this person to go out of the room while the rest of the class decide on the character.) Put a paper hat on the person with the character's name written on it or get the person to sit with his or her back to the board, then write the character's name on the board.

The person has to start by asking questions to find out who he or she is. The person can only ask questions that require 'yes' or 'no' answers. The class can only answer **ya**, **tidak**, **bukan** or **belum**. No other information should be given. The person cannot ask, for example, 'What is my profession?' or 'Where do I live?'. Here are some examples of such questions.

Person A: **Saya orang?**
Am I a person?
Class: **Ya.**
Yes.
Person A: **Apakah saya laki-laki?**
Am I male?
Class: **Bukan.**
No.
Person A: **Saya sudah pernah ke Australia?**
Have I been to (= visited) Australia?
Class: **Belum.**
Not yet.

You can go on as long as you like with one person or limit the number of questions and, if the person cannot find out the identity of his or her character, he or she has to sit down.

Positive answers with *mau, sudah, boleh* or *bisa*

Mau, **sudah**, **boleh** and **bisa** are used in answers to questions that also contain them. **Mau** expresses a want or wish; **sudah** indicates that an action has been completed (the opposite of **belum**); **boleh** shows permission; **bisa** shows capability or permission, depending on the context. When used as permission, **bisa** means the same as **boleh**. These words are sometimes preceded by **ya** or **iya** when used as an answer.

A: **Mau makan?**
Do you want to eat? (Notice that the subject 'you' is often not mentioned in Indonesian.)
B: **Iya, mau.**
Yes, I do.

A: **Kamu sudah mandi?**
Have you bathed?
B: **Sudah.**
Yes, I have.

A: **Boleh/bisa saya pinjam topinya?**
May/can I borrow the hat? (= your hat) → permission
B: **Ya, boleh/bisa.**
Yes, you may/can.

A: **Bisa kita keluar lewat sini?**
Can we go out this way? → capability
B: **Ya, bisa.**
Yes, you can.

To emphasise a positive answer, we can add the word **saja** after **mau**, **boleh** or **bisa** (but not after **sudah**).

A: **Boleh makan kuenya?**
Can I eat the cake? ('I' is not mentioned.)
B: **Ya, boleh saja.**
Yes, of course.

A: **Mau jalan-jalan?**
Do you want to go for a walk? ('You' is not mentioned.)
B: **Ya, mau saja.**
Yes, of course.

It is common to further emphasise the answer by reduplicating the answer word, followed by **saja**. This is not applicable to **belum**.

A: **Bisa pinjam CD-nya?**
Can I borrow the CD? (= your CD)
B: **Iya, bisa-bisa saja.**
Yes, of course you can.

A: **Kamu mau kopi?**
Would you like a coffee?
B: **Ya, mau-mau saja.**
Yes, of course I would.

LATIHAN 5

Work in pairs, taking turns to ask and answer the following questions in Indonesian. The (+) symbol means that the answer must be positive; the (-) symbol means that the answer must be negative.

Note
If you interview your teacher, do not use **kamu**. Rather, you should say '**Bu** + her name' or '**Pak** + his name'.

1 **A:** Murid boleh merokok di sekolah ini?
B: (+)
2 **A:** Kamu mau belajar bahasa Indonesia di Jakarta?
B: (+)
3 **A:** Boleh bapak saya pinjam mobilmu?
B: (-)
4 **A:** Kamu pernah ke Spanyol?
B: (+)
5 **A:** Kamu menelepon saya kemarin?
B: (-)
6 **A:** Kamu sudah mandi?
B: (-)
7 **A:** Adikmu mau ayam goreng ini?
B: (-)
8 **A:** Pagi ini kamu sudah makan?
B: (+)
9 **A:** Apakah kamu pernah mencoba makan durian?
B: (+)
10 **A:** Menurut anda, harga mobil itu mahal atau tidak?
B: (+)

KOSAKATA

mencoba	to try
menurut	according to
pernah	have been to, have ever

LATIHAN 6

Conduct a survey among your classmates to find out their habits, likes and dislikes. Copy the following tables, turning the information in the left column of each table into questions. Then interview five people, asking them the questions that you have prepared, and record their responses.

Kesukaan: makanan dan minuman
Favourites: food and drink

	TEMAN 1	TEMAN 2	TEMAN 3	TEMAN 4	TEMAN 5
banyak makan buah-buahan eat a lot of fruit					
sering makan pizza often eat pizza					
banyak minum susu drink a lot of milk					
sering makan es krim often eat icecream					

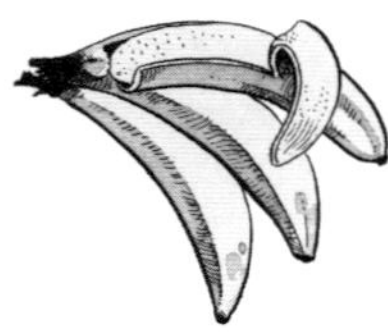

Kebiasaan di rumah
Habits at home

	TEMAN 1	TEMAN 2	TEMAN 3	TEMAN 4	TEMAN 5
suka menonton televisi like watching television					
membersihkan kamar sendiri clean own room					
membantu cuci piring help do the dishes					
mencuci baju sendiri wash own clothes					
sering membaca surat kabar often read newspaper					

Make up five more questions of your own to find out more about your classmates' likes and dislikes.

Summary

- Asking questions:
  —with raised intonation
  —with **apa(kah)**
  —using tags **bukan**, **kan** or **ya**
  —using question words:
  apa, **siapa**, **berapa**, **keberapa**, **kapan**, **bila** (formal), **bagaimana**, **di mana**, **ke mana**, **dari mana**, **mengapa**, **kenapa** (informal), **untuk apa**
  (Remember: **kapan** and **bila** are used only in questions, not as conjunctions.)
- Negative answers:
  —**bukan** for nouns
  —**tidak** for verbs, adjectives and adverbs
  —**belum** for action not yet performed or completed
- Positive answers:
  —**ya** or **iya** for a simple 'yes'
  —**mau** for want or wish
  —**boleh** for giving permission
  —**bisa** for either permission or capability
  —**sudah** for action already performed or completed
  —the addition of **saja** or reduplicated word + **saja** to emphasise the answer (not applicable for **sudah**)

2

Noun Phrases

In this chapter we will learn about how a noun can combine with other words. For example:

<u>baju</u> biru	blue <u>shirt</u>
<u>guru</u> saya	my <u>teacher</u>
<u>murid</u> itu	that <u>student</u>

These combinations of words are called *phrases.*

A phrase is a meaningful group of words, one of which is usually the main word (technically called the *head*). A phrase in which the head is a noun is called a *noun phrase.*

In Indonesian noun phrases, the head comes before the other word(s), while in English it is generally the other way round. Here are the combinations that you will find in Indonesian:

- noun + possessor
- noun + another noun
- noun + adjective
- noun + verb

For simplicity, head nouns are referred to as nouns throughout the rest of this chapter, and they are underlined for easy identification.

2.1 Noun + possessor

In this type of noun phrase, the noun refers to something that belongs to a person or animal. For instance, in **<u>buku</u> Nina** (Nina's book) below, a book is being referred to, so the word **buku** comes first. **Nina** (name of a person) specifies to whom the book belongs, so it is placed after the noun. Similarly, in **<u>ayah</u> saya** (my father), 'father' is being referred to, and the word 'my' specifies that the father belongs to you, so **ayah** comes first and **saya** after.

NOUN	POSSESSOR (WHO THE THING BELONGS TO)	ENGLISH MEANING
buku	**Nina**	
book	Nina	Nina's book
ayah	**saya**	
father	my	my father
kantor	**Pak Rudi**	
office	Mr Rudi	Mr Rudi's office
mobil	**mereka**	
car	their	their car
ekor	**anjing**	
tail	dog	dog's tail

You can build more complex noun phrases of this kind by adding another noun in front of the phrase. Remember that the thing to which you are referring always comes first. For instance, when you say 'my father's car', it is a car to which you are referring, so the word **mobil** comes first, followed by **ayah saya**.

NOUN	NOUN + POSSESSOR	ENGLISH MEANING
mobil	**ayah saya**	
car	my father	my father's car
buku	**ibu Nina**	
book	Nina's mother	Nina's mother's book
ekor	**anjing saya**	
tail	my dog	my dog's tail

LATIHAN 1

Here are some pictures of people and objects. Write the Indonesian equivalents of the English noun phrases provided.

1 Their computer

2 My friend

3 Tini's teacher's house

2.2 Noun + another noun

In this type of noun phrase, the second noun is also related to the head noun, but not as a possessor as in the above. The second noun may specify the location mentioned in the head, such as 'school <u>library</u>' (library located at a school) or 'football <u>field</u>' (a field for playing football), or give other specifications.

NOUN	ANOTHER NOUN	ENGLISH MEANING
<u>perpustakaan</u> library	**sekolah** school	school <u>library</u>
<u>lapangan</u> field	**sepak bola** football	football <u>field</u>
<u>sampul</u> cover	**buku** book	book <u>cover</u>
<u>merek</u> brand	**komputer** computer	computer <u>brand name</u>

Did you know?
The word for 'glove' in Indonesian is:

<u>Kaos</u>	**tangan**	
Stretch fabric	hand	→ glove

LATIHAN 2

Write the Indonesian equivalents of the English noun phrases describing these pictures.

1 Post office

2 Movie theatre

3 Rubbish bin

2.3 Noun + adjective

In this type of noun phrase, the adjective that follows the noun describes such things as the size, colour, taste or, generally, the quality of the thing referred to by the noun.

NOUN	ADJECTIVE	ENGLISH MEANING
rumah	**besar**	
house	big	big house
sepeda	**kecil**	
bicycle	small	small bicycle
balon	**hijau**	
balloon	green	green balloon
teh	**manis**	
tea	sweet	sweet tea
rumah	**sakit**	
house	sick	hospital (literally 'house for the sick')

2.4 Noun + verb

When the noun is followed by a verb, the verb indicates the activity for which the noun is used.

NOUN	VERB	ENGLISH MEANING
rumah	**makan**	
house	eat	eating house, restaurant
gedung	**olahraga**	
hall	sport	sports hall
kamar	**mandi**	
room	bath	bathroom
papan	**tulis**	
board	to write	blackboard/whiteboard
tempat	**tidur**	
place	to sleep	place to sleep → bed

We can also add an adjective to the phrase.

NOUN + VERB	ADJECTIVE	ENGLISH MEANING
rumah makan	**mahal**	
restaurant	expensive	expensive restaurant
gedung olahraga	**megah**	
sports hall	grand	grand sports hall
kamar mandi	**kotor**	
bathroom	dirty	dirty bathroom

2.5 Noun + demonstrative

A *demonstrative* is a word that can be used to point at something, such as **ini** (this) and **itu** (that). In this type of noun phrase, the demonstrative is placed after the noun.

NOUN	DEMONSTRATIVE	ENGLISH MEANING
universitas	**itu**	
university	that	that university
kotak	**ini**	
box	this	this box

To form more complex noun phrases, you can combine any of the above noun phrases with the demonstrative.

NOUN + POSSESSOR	DEMONSTRATIVE	ENGLISH MEANING
mobil ayah saya	**ini**	
my father's car	this	this car of my father's
perpustakaan sekolah	**itu**	
school library	that	that school library
rumah besar	**ini**	
big house	this	this big house
rumah makan mahal	**itu**	
expensive restaurant	that	that expensive eating house/restaurant

Note

Ini and **itu** can also be placed *before* a noun phrase to mean 'this is/was' or 'these are/were'.

Ini rumah saya.
This is my house.

Itu kantor pos.
That is the post office.

LATIHAN 3

Below are noun phrases that are *noun + adjective*, *noun + verb* and *noun + demonstrative*. Translate each phrase into Indonesian. You may need to consult your dictionary for this exercise.

1 This apple
2 Bedroom (in Indonesian, literally 'sleeping room')
3 These students
4 Those bicycles
5 Brown eyes
6 Restaurant (in Indonesian, literally 'eating house')

LATIHAN 4

Translate the following more complex noun phrases into Indonesian, working your way from right to left. You may need to consult your dictionary for this exercise.

Example:

That yellow door:	**Pintu**	**kuning**	**itu**
	door	yellow	that

1 My favourite song
2 Big round hat
3 Small red bird
4 Delicious fried rice
5 Black long pants

LATIHAN 5

One way of forming simple sentences in Indonesian is by combining complex noun phrases with an adjective or another noun. Write simple sentences by finding the Indonesian equivalent of the noun phrases and the adjectives below. Your sentences will have this structure: *complex noun phrase* + *adjective* or *complex noun phrase* + *noun*.

Example:

Complex noun phrase		Adjective
Their big house	→	new
Rumah besar mereka	→	**baru**

Rumah besar mereka baru = Their big house is new.

Notice that in simple sentences like this, the word 'is' need not be translated into Indonesian. When you read the sentence, though, you will need to give a short pause where the arrow is.

1	Her sports shoes	→	expensive
2	Their large bathroom	→	green
3	That movie theatre	→	small
4	My motorbike	→	Honda
5	My mother's name	→	Jane

LATIHAN 6

Now that you know how to form simple and complex noun phrases and also how to write some simple sentences, try to give a simple description in Indonesian of a person or an object by using similar forms. The models below are provided to help you write your own descriptions. The noun phrases are underlined.

Present your description orally to the class. Remember to pause after the noun phrase.

1 Description of oneself:

<u>Nama saya</u> Intan.

My name is Intan.

Umur saya 20 tahun.
My age is 20 years. → I am 20 years old.
Kota kelahiran saya Melbourne.
My birthplace is Melbourne.
Makanan kesukaan saya nasi goreng dan sambal.
My favourite food is fried rice and chilli sauce.

2 Description of a pet:
Nama kucing saya Manis.
My cat's name is Manis.
Warna bulu Manis putih.
The colour of Manis's fur is white.
Makanan kesukaan Manis ikan goreng.
Manis's favourite food is fried fish.
Umur Manis 20 bulan.
Manis's age is 20 months. → Manis is 20 months old.

Summary

- Noun phrases can be:
  —*noun* + *possessor*; for example, **topi saya**
  —*noun* + *another noun*; for example, **rumah makan**
  —*noun* + *adjective*; for example, **rumah besar**
  —*noun* + *verb*; for example, **kamar mandi**
- Remember that, as a general rule, the thing to which you are referring comes first and everything else comes after it. When translating complex noun phrases from English, work your way from right to left.

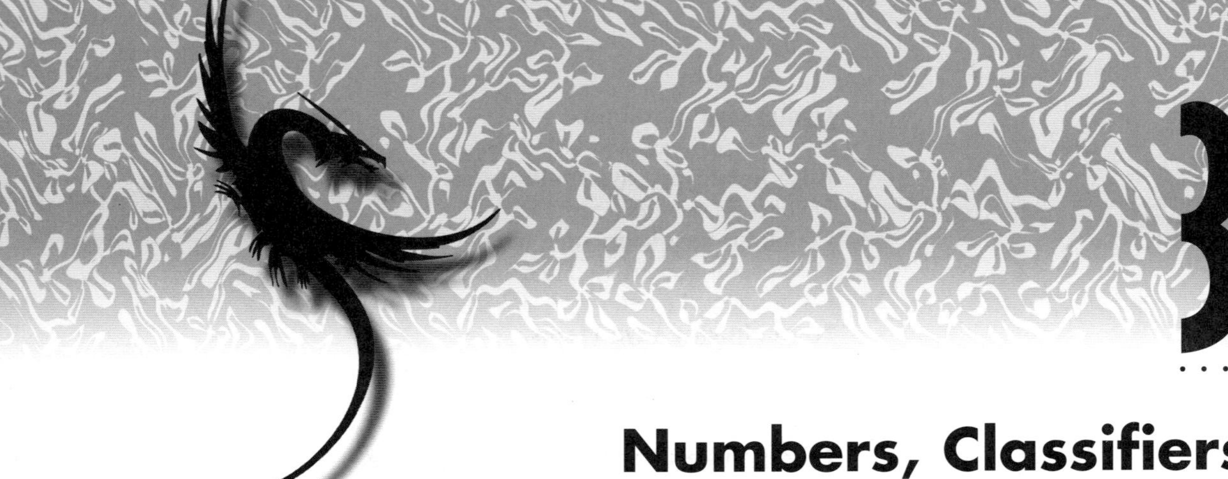

3 Numbers, Classifiers and Quantity

3.1 Numbers

Cardinal and ordinal numbers

Cardinal numbers are those we use for counting things (for example, one, two, three, one hundred), while ordinal numbers are those we use to say things in sequence. The tables below show how these two kinds of numbers are expressed in Indonesian.

NUMBERS 1–10

CARDINAL NUMBERS	ORDINAL NUMBERS Add prefix **ke-** to the cardinal number (except ***pertama** = first)
0: **nol**	-
1: **satu**	1st: ***pertama** (not **kesatu**)
2: **dua**	2nd: **kedua**
3: **tiga**	3rd: **ketiga**
4: **empat**	4th: **keempat**
5: **lima**	5th: **kelima**
6: **enam**	6th: **keenam**
7: **tujuh**	7th: **ketujuh**
8: **delapan**	8th: **kedelapan**
9: **sembilan**	9th: **kesembilan**
10: **sepuluh**	10th: **kesepuluh**

NUMBERS 11–20

CARDINAL NUMBERS *For '-teen' add **belas***	ORDINAL NUMBERS Add prefix **ke-** to the cardinal number
11: **sebelas**	11th: **kesebelas**
12: **dua belas**	12th: **kedua belas**
13: **tiga belas**	13th: **ketiga belas**
14: **empat belas**	14th: **keempat belas**
15: **lima belas**	15th: **kelima belas**
16: **enam belas**	16th: **keenam belas**
17: **tujuh belas**	17th: **ketujuh belas**
18: **delapan belas**	18th: **kedelapan belas**
19: **sembilan belas**	19th: **kesembilan belas**
20: **dua puluh**	20th: **kedua puluh**

NUMBERS IN THE MULTIPLICATION OF TENS

CARDINAL NUMBERS *Add **puluh*** *(see also 10 and 20 above)*	ORDINAL NUMBERS Add prefix **ke-** to the cardinal number
30: **tiga puluh**	30th: **ketiga puluh**
40: **empat puluh**	40th: **keempat puluh**
60: **enam puluh**	60th: **keenam puluh**
80: **delapan puluh**	80th: **kedelapan puluh**
90: **sembilan puluh**	90th: **kesembilan puluh**

BIGGER NUMBERS

hundred: **ratus**
thousand: **ribu**
million: **juta**
billion: **miliar**

Note
The prefix **se-** in numbers means 'one' (but it is not used for the number 1), hence:

sepuluh	(one ten)	10
sebelas	(one teen)	11
seratus	(one hundred)	100
seribu	(one thousand)	1000
sejuta	(one million)	1000.000
semiliar	(one billion)	1000.000.000

To say some big numbers, follow the pattern shown below.

3500: 3000 = tiga ribu
500 = lima ratus
→ tiga ribu lima ratus

6750: 6000 = enam ribu
700 = tujuh ratus
50 = lima puluh
→ enam ribu tujuh ratus lima puluh

1.450.500: 1000.000.000 = sejuta
450.000 = empat ratus lima puluh ribu
500 = lima ratus
→ sejuta empat ratus lima puluh ribu lima ratus

Did you know?
A soccer team in Indonesian is called **kesebelasan** (the eleven) because there are eleven people in a team.

LATIHAN 1

Can you say the following numbers in Indonesian?

1 15
2 310
3 564
4 2701
5 7550
6 1683
7 87.575
8 10.950
9 33.845
10 1.250.000

LATIHAN 2

How do you say the following in Indonesian? Say the non-number word first, then the ordinal number. You may need to consult your dictionary for this exercise.

Example:
Eighth person
Orang kedelapan

1 Twenty-first century
2 Seventeenth birthday
3 First child
4 Fifth month
5 Second day
6 Third book
7 Tenth film
8 Fifth president
9 One thousandth print
10 Second car

Ke-: 'the + number'

The prefix **ke-** followed by a number, as in ordinal numbers, can also be used to mean 'the + number'. In this case, **ke-** is attached to the number, then followed by the noun.

ketiga anak itu
the three children

kedua guru itu
the two teachers
(both teachers)

Kelima mahasiswa itu mengambil mata kuliah Antropologi.
The five university students take Anthropology as their subject.

Keempat temannya sudah pindah ke kota lain.
The four of his/her friends have moved to another city.

We can omit the noun if it is already understood or mentioned before. However, we need to add **-nya** after **ke** + number.

Keduanya laki-laki.
Both are boys. → (referring to children)

Ketiganya tidak mau bicara.
The three of them did not want to talk.

Sometimes the number is reduplicated for emphasis.

Ketiga-tiganya tidak mau bicara.
All three of them did not want to talk.

Fractions

The Indonesian word for 'fractions' is **angka pecahan**, which literally means 'broken number'. To say 'one ...th', the prefix **seper-** is added to the number, except for 'half', which is prefixed by **se-**.

setengah	one-half
sepertiga	one-third
seperempat	one-quarter
seperdelapan	one-eighth
seperseratus	one-hundredth

For other fractions, add **per-** only to the larger number and place the smaller number before it.

dua pertiga	two-thirds
dua perseratus	two-hundredths

Did you know?
The word **tengah** 'half, middle' can be used to form other nouns.

pertengahan	middle (usually for calendar time)
pertengahan bulan	middle of the month
pertengahan tahun	middle of the year
tengah hari	middle of the day; midday
tengah jalan	middle of the road

Likewise, we can also form other nouns from the numbers **tiga** and **empat**.

pertigaan	T-intersection
perempatan	crossroad

LATIHAN 3

Say the following fractions in Indonesian.

1 $\frac{5}{8}$
2 $\frac{1}{10}$
3 $7\frac{1}{2}$
4 $\frac{1}{6}$
5 $\frac{2}{8}$
6 $1\frac{3}{4}$
7 $\frac{1}{5}$
8 $6\frac{2}{3}$
9 $9\frac{1}{2}$
10 $8\frac{3}{4}$

3.2 Classifiers

Classifiers are words that are used to group things in the world (according to shape, number, size and so on). Many languages have classifiers, including English. For example:

a bar of soap or chocolate
a bunch of flowers
a flock of sheep
a herd of cattle

Classifiers are used to classify, not only those things that the words literally stand for, but also other things. For example, in Indonesian **ekor** literally means 'tail'; but the word is used as a classifier for animals that have tails as well as for those that do not.

batang	literally 'log' (for example, for timber, pencil, stick)
buah	literally 'fruit' (for example, for bicycle, car, computer, essay, book)
ekor	literally 'tail' (for example, for all animals)
helai	literally 'sheet' (for example, for paper, pieces of clothing, fabric)
orang	literally 'person' (for example, for people, such as teacher, student)
potong	literally 'cut' (for example, for pieces of clothing, sliced things, cut-up things)
sisir	literally 'comb' (for example, for a hand of bananas)

As in English, we use these classifiers by putting in the number first, followed by the classifier, then the noun. Notice below that the prefix **se-** for 'one' is attached to the classifier; any other number is written separately.

se+batang	**pohon**			
one+classifier	tree	→	a tree	
dua	**ekor**	**kucing**		
number	classifier	thing	→	two cats

To ask questions with classifiers, use **berapa**, followed by the classifier, then the noun.

Berapa batang pohon?
How many trees?

5 batang.
Five.

Berapa ekor kucing?
How many cats?

Dua ekor.
Two.

Be careful!
When we use **se-** with a classifier to mean 'one', it must be attached to the classifier, not the noun. We cannot say, for example:

sesapi	a cow
sebuku	a book

LATIHAN 4

Use classifiers to identify the following things in Indonesian.

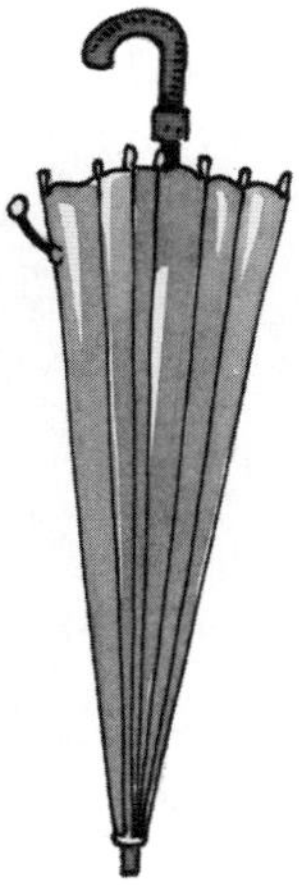

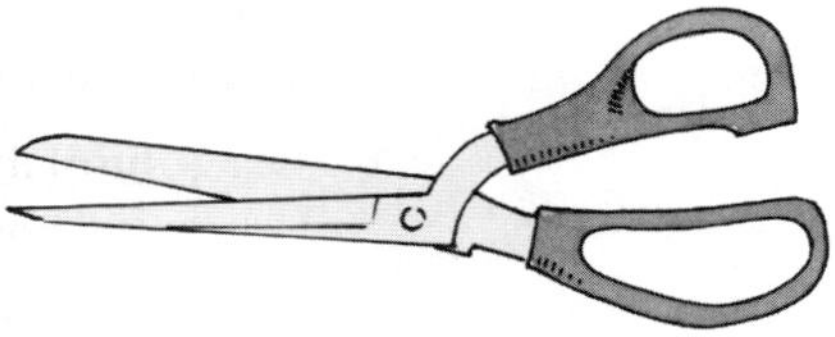

3.3 Quantity

To show quantity, we can use the following words.

- **banyak**
- **sedikit**
- **beberapa**
- **kurang lebih**
- **jumlah**

Banyak and *sedikit*

To say 'many, much, a lot', use **banyak**. This word can be used for things that are countable, such as people and books, as well as for things that are not countable, such as water and sugar.

Banyak orang datang ke rapat itu.
Many people came to that meeting.

Tolong beri banyak sambal ya.
Please give a lot of sambal (chilli paste).

To say 'a little' or 'few', use **sedikit**. Like **banyak**, we can use this word both for countable and uncountable things.

Saya suka minum teh dengan sedikit gula.
I like drinking tea with a little sugar.

Murid di kelas ini hanya sedikit.
The students in this class are few.

Beberapa

To say 'a few, a number of', use **beberapa**.

Beberapa pekerja dipecat karena ketahuan mencuri uang.
A number of workers were fired because they were caught stealing money.

Kurang lebih

Kurang lebih literally means 'less, more' and is used to say 'approximately'.

Panjang meja ini kurang lebih satu setengah meter.
The length of this table is approximately one and a half metres.

Jumlah

Jumlah means 'total, the total number of'.

Jumlah wartawan yang ke sana dua puluh orang.
The total number of journalists who went there was twenty.

3.4 Group words

- **sekelompok**
- **sekumpulan**
- **sepasang**
- **segelintir**

Sekelompok and *sekumpulan*

Sekelompok and **sekumpulan** both mean 'a group of' or 'a bunch of'.

> **Sekelompok penjahat berhasil merampok bank itu.**
> A group of criminals succeeded in robbing that bank.
>
> **Sekumpulan murid dari Jakarta berkunjung ke Sydney bulan lalu.**
> A group of students from Jakarta visited Sydney last month.

Sepasang

Sepasang means 'a pair of' or 'a couple of'.

> **Kemarin ibu membeli sepasang sepatu.**
> Yesterday mother bought a pair of shoes.

Segelintir

Segelintir literally means 'a pellet'. It is usually used to refer to a small number of people. It is informal and is used to emphasise the fact that the number is small.

> **Diskusi itu hanya dihadiri segelintir orang.**
> That discussion was attended by only very few people.

LATIHAN 5

KOSAKATA

anting-anting	earrings
bertambah	to increase
cepat gemuk	to put on weight quickly
hadiah	present, gift
sepak bola	football
tewas	to die (in an accident, disaster or battlefield)
ulang tahun	birthday
wisatawan	tourist

Choose the correct alternative to complete each sentence.

1 Untuk hadiah ulang tahun, saya mendapat ... anting-anting.
- **a** satu
- **b** sepasang
- **c** sebuah

2 ... wisatawan yang ke Indonesia bertambah setiap tahun.
- **a** Beberapa
- **b** Segelintir
- **c** Jumlah

3 Setiap hari Tuti makan ... supaya cepat gemuk.
- **a** sedikit
- **b** banyak
- **c** kurang lebih

4 Jumlah orang yang tewas ... 500 orang.
- **a** kurang lebih
- **b** total
- **c** banyak

5 … anak-anak berlari-lari di lapangan sepak bola.
  a Jumlah
  b Kurang lebih
  c Sekelompok

Summary

- Cardinal numbers: **se-** means 'one' (for example, **sepuluh**, **sebelas**)
- Ordinal numbers: add **ke-** to cardinal numbers
- Fractions: shown by **per-** (for example, **sepertiga** = one-third)
- Classifiers: **batang**, **buah**, **ekor**, **helai**, **orang**, **potong**, **sisir** + noun (or noun phrase)
- Quantity: **banyak**, **sedikit**, **beberapa**, **kurang lebih**, **jumlah**
- Group words: **sekelompok**, **sekumpulan**, **sepasang**, **segelintir**

4

Saying 'To Be' with *Adalah* and *Ialah*

In this chapter we will learn how to say 'to be', which, in English, is conveyed by 'am', is, are, was, were' (for example, 'I am a student', 'They were there'). In Indonesian, we use the following words.

- **adalah**
- **ialah**

Dia adalah petenis.
He/she is a tennis player.

Mereka ialah murid sekolah menengah.
They are high school students.

4.1 The difference between *adalah* and *ialah*

The difference between **adalah** and **ialah** is that **ialah** cannot be used for first person 'I' (**saya**, **aku**, **kami**) or second person 'you' (**anda**, **kamu**, **Saudara**, **kalian**). We cannot say, for instance:

Saya ialah murid.
I am a student.

Kamu ialah teman kami.
You are our friends.

Instead, we should say:

Saya adalah murid.
I am a student.

Kamu adalah teman kami.
You are our friends.

LATIHAN 1

Choose the correct answer in each of the following sentences. Remember that **ialah** is not for first and second persons. Remember also that in other cases both **adalah** and **ialah** are acceptable.

KOSAKATA

bijaksana	wise
dosen	lecturer
ikan air tawar	freshwater fish
kegemaran	hobby
penyiar	broadcaster
pertama	first
petani	farmer
telepon genggam	mobile phone

1 Bapaknya **adalah/ialah** petani.
2 Yanti **adalah/ialah** seorang penyiar radio.
3 Ikan-ikan ini **adalah/ialah** ikan air tawar.
4 Telepon genggam saya **adalah/ialah** dari ibu saya.
5 Kami **adalah/ialah** murid-murid sekolah itu.
6 Bu Sofia **adalah/ialah** dosen Universitas Indonesia di Jakarta.
7 Saya **adalah/ialah** anak pertama di keluarga saya.
8 Film itu **adalah/ialah** film horor.
9 Kegemaran ibu saya **adalah/ialah** bersepeda pada hari minggu.
10 Anda **adalah/ialah** orang yang bijaksana.

4.2 The function of *adalah* and *ialah*

The main function of **adalah** and **ialah** is to link one part of a sentence to another. The first part of the sentence is called the *subject*, while the other part is the *predicate*.

SUBJECT	*ADALAH/IALAH*	PREDICATE
Orang itu	**adalah/ialah**	**Paman saya.**
That person	is	my uncle.
Kue itu	**adalah/ialah**	**kue apel.**
That cake	is	apple cake.
Sepeda ini	**adalah/ialah**	**sepeda balap.**
This bike	is	a racing bike.

We can also put an adjective or prepositional phrase (for example, 'for you', 'from Malaysia', 'in class') in the predicate slot.

SUBJECT	*ADALAH/IALAH*	PREDICATE
Pengumuman itu	**adalah/ialah**	**penting.**
That announcement	is	important.
Hadiah ini	**adalah/ialah**	**untuk kamu.**
This present	is	for you.
Teman saya Halimah	**adalah/ialah**	**dari Malaysia.**
My friend Halimah	is	from Malaysia.

4.3 Optional *adalah* and *ialah*

Adalah and **ialah** are mostly optional. We can omit them altogether if we wish to. In fact, in casual conversation people hardly use these words. This is different from English, where 'to be' is essential in the sentences we looked at. So why learn **adalah** and **ialah**, you might ask. The answer is simply that we are likely to come across these words in written and in formal spoken Indonesian. They are also appropriate for when you want to write essays in Indonesian.

Here are some examples of sentences without **adalah** and **ialah**.

Saya dari Australia.
I am from Australia.

Hadiah ini untuk kamu.
This present is for you.

4.4 *Merupakan*

There is another word in Indonesian for 'to be'; namely, **merupakan**. This word is used to describe or define the phrase in the earlier part of the sentence.

Menjadi presiden merupakan pekerjaan yang tidak mudah.
Literally: Being a president is a job that is not easy.
→ Being a president is not an easy job.

Olahraga merupakan kegiatan yang menyehatkan.
Literally: Playing sport is an activity that is healthy.
→ Playing sport is a healthy activity.

LATIHAN 2

Copy and complete the sentences, filling in the empty spaces.

SUBJECT	*ADALAH OR IALAH*	PREDICATE
1 Orang buta itu		
2 Kanguru		
3		binatang laut.
4		barang mahal.
5	adalah	
6	ialah	
7 Sabuk kulit ini		
8 Tiket ini		
9		tidak baik untuk kesehatan.
10		dari penggemarnya.

KOSAKATA

barang	goods
buta	blind
kesehatan	health
penggemar	fan
sabuk kulit	leather belt

LATIHAN 3

Match the words on the left with those on the right and link them by using either **adalah** or **ialah**.

KOSAKATA

buatan	make (noun)
cita-cita	dream, aspiration
gedung	building
orang asing	foreigner
pasta gigi	toothpaste
Sekolah Dasar	Primary School
tetangga	neighbour

SUBJECT	*ADALAH* OR *IALAH*	PREDICATE
1 Pohon itu		**a** dari teman saya di Medan.
2 Orang asing itu		**b** iklan pasta gigi.
3 Gedung tinggi itu		**c** menjadi astronaut.
4 Email ini		**d** anak Pak Rudi.
5 Adik perempuan saya		**e** pohon mangga.
6 Penjual rokok itu		**f** hotel Borobudur.
7 Iklan bagus itu		**g** dari Itali.
8 Cita-cita saya		**h** murid Sekolah Dasar.
9 Tetangga saya		**i** orang yang sangat baik.
10 Mobil itu		**j** buatan Jerman.

Summary

- **Adalah** and **ialah** both mean 'to be' and are interchangeable. The difference is, **ialah** may not be used for first or second persons.
- **Adalah** and **ialah** are optional. People rarely use them in casual conversation; they are more suitable for writing and when speaking in formal settings.
- **Merupakan** also means 'to be'. It is used to describe or define the preceding phrase.

5

Prepositions

Prepositions are words that are usually placed before a noun or pronoun. Some examples in English are 'on', 'in', 'at', 'to', 'from', 'along', 'around', 'before' and 'after'.

5.1 Basic prepositions

- **di** (on, in, at)
- **ke** (to)
- **dari** (from)

Ibu membaca sambil duduk <u>di</u> kursi.
Mother is reading while sitting <u>on</u> the chair.

Ali berlari <u>ke</u> stasiun untuk mengejar kereta.
Ali is running <u>to</u> the station to catch the train.

Teman saya Julie berasal <u>dari</u> Canberra.
My friend Julie is originally <u>from</u> Canberra.

Belanjaan ada <u>di dalam</u> keranjang belanja.
The shopping is <u>inside</u> the shopping trolley.

After **di**, **ke** and **dari** we can add another word to make the location more specific. These are words such as **atas**, **bawah**, **depan** and **belakang**, as shown below. When we combine **di**, **ke** or **dari** with any of these words, we get *compound prepositions*. Some equivalents in English are 'on top of', 'in (the) back of' and 'out of'.

PREPOSITION	ENGLISH MEANING
di atas	on top of, above
di bawah	under, below
di belakang	behind
di depan	in front of
di dekat	near
di dalam	inside
di luar	outside
di sebelah	beside
di sekitar	around, within the vicinity of
di sepanjang	along

Ada makanan dan minuman di atas meja.
There is food and drink on top of the table.
(In English, we usually say 'There is food and drink on the table'.)

Kecap manis ada di dalam lemari.
The sweet soy sauce is inside the cupboard.

Anak-anak berlarian di sepanjang koridor.
Children are running along the corridor.

Ada banyak taman di sekitar rumah saya.
There are many parks around my house.

Ke is often used to mean 'to go to' even though the word **pergi** (go) is not mentioned.

PREPOSITION	ENGLISH MEANING
ke dalam	to go inside, inward
ke luar	to go outside, outward
ke belakang	to go to the back
ke bawah	to go down, downward
ke atas	to go up, upward
ke sebelah	to go to the side

Keluarga Sutomo akan ke Surabaya minggu depan.
The Sutomo family will be going to Surabaya next week.

Maaf, saya mau ke luar sebentar.
Excuse me, I want to go outside for a short while.

Did you know?
Ke belakang also means 'to go to the toilet'. So, to say to your teacher that you want to go to the toilet, you would say **Maaf Bu/Pak, boleh saya ke belakang?** (Excuse me, Miss/Sir, can I go to the toilet?).

LATIHAN 1

Choose one of the prepositions below for each of the sentences. There is only one answer for each sentence.

KOSAKATA

berasal	to come from
jangan	don't
lemari	wardrobe
memasukkan	to put into
ruangan	room
taman	park
taruh	to put

dari	**di luar**	**ke belakang**	**di dalam**	**ke**
di belakang	**di dekat**	**di sebelah**	**di atas**	**ke dalam**

1 Di mana kamu taruh kopi saya? ______________ meja.
2 Banyak ikan besar dan kecil ______________ akuarium itu.
3 Akhir minggu ini kami akan pergi ______________ Taman Safari.
4 Ada toko buku ______________ kantor pos.
5 ______________ rumah saya ada taman besar.
6 Kofi berasal ______________ Tanzania.
7 Silakan merokok ______________, jangan di dalam ruangan ini.

8 Banyak pohon mangga tumbuh ________________________ rumah saya.
9 Maaf Pak, boleh saya ________________________?
10 Roni memasukkan pakaiannya ________________________ lemari.

LATIHAN 2

KOSAKATA

babi pig
bebek duck
gereja church
lampu lalu lintas traffic light
mesjid mosque
pesawat terbang aeroplane

Work in pairs to ask each other where the following things are. Start your question with **di mana** (where). Try to answer using either simple or compound prepositions.

Example:

Di mana mesjid itu?
Di jalan Melati, di belakang gereja.

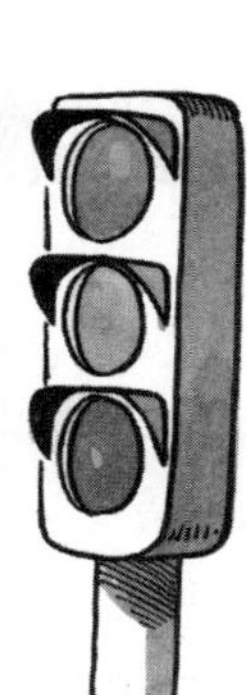

5.2 Other prepositions

- **pada** (on, at)
- **kepada** (to, at, with)

The prepositions **pada** and **kepada** are often used for abstract things and people.

Pada: on, at (for time, abstract things or people)

Kereta api ini akan berangkat pada jam 10 pagi.
This train will depart at 10 a.m.

Kepada: to, at or with a person

Murid-murid menulis surat kepada sahabat pena mereka di Indonesia.
The students are writing a letter to their penfriends in Indonesia.

Emotions are abstract things and you will find that **pada** and **kepada** often appear with such verbs. In English, often we do not need to put a preposition with these verbs; however, in Indonesian, we do (at least when we speak in standard Indonesian). Notice the difference between English and Indonesian in the following sentences.

ENGLISH	INDONESIAN
I love you.	**Aku cinta (ke)padamu.** Literally: 'I love at/with you.'
They hate him.	**Mereka benci (ke)pada dia.** or **Mereka benci (ke)padanya.** Literally: 'They hate at him.'

Other expressions of emotion, however, are similar to English in the sense that a preposition is required.

ENGLISH	INDONESIAN
I am afraid of her.	**Saya takut (ke)pada dia.** or **Saya takut (ke)padanya.**
They are angry with us.	**Mereka marah (ke)pada kita.**

LATIHAN 3

Below are some more emotion verbs in English. Write a simple sentence with each of them in Indonesian. Remember to use the preposition **pada** or **kepada** in each sentence. You may need to consult your dictionary for this exercise.

1 To be embarrassed in front of someone
2 To be annoyed with someone
3 To like someone
4 To be fond of someone
5 To miss someone (to long for someone)

Here are some more prepositions that are useful for us to know.

- **selama** (during, for the duration of)
- **sampai** (until, up to)
- **sebelum** (before)
- **sesudah** (after)

Selama: during, for the duration of

Kakak perempuan saya akan pergi ke luar kota selama tiga hari.
My older sister will go out of town for three days.

Sampai: until, up to

Liburan akhir tahun adalah dari tanggal 20 Desember <u>sampai</u> 31 Januari.
The end-of-year holiday is from 20 Desember <u>until</u> 31 January.

Handy expression
Sampai mana tadi? means 'where were we/they up to?' You can use this expression, for example, when telling a story and you are interrupted; you want to continue, but forget where you were up to.

Sudah sampai mana? means 'where have we/they got to?' You can use this expression, for example, when you are travelling and want to know where you are in relation to your destination.

Sebelum: before

Sikatlah gigimu <u>sebelum</u> tidur malam.
Brush your teeth <u>before</u> going to bed at night.

Sesudah: after

Kamu boleh menonton televisi <u>sesudah</u> selesai pekerjaan rumahmu.
You may watch television <u>after</u> finishing your homework.

LATIHAN 4

Choose a suitable preposition (other than the basic prepositions) for each of the following sentences.

1 Rani menulis surat ______________________ sahabat penanya di Turki.
2 Setiap pagi kami bangun ______________________ jam 7.
3 Saya cinta sekali ______________________ ibu dan bapak saya.
4 Kami akan makan siang ______________________ kelas ini selesai.
5 Indra tinggal di London ______________________ 3 tahun.
6 Jangan marah ______________________ saya.
7 Berpikir dulu ______________________ bertindak.
8 Di Indonesia murid-murid ke sekolah dari hari Senin ______________________ hari Sabtu.
9 Siapa yang benci ______________________ kamu?
10 Murid-murid suka sekali ______________________ cerita lucu itu.

KOSAKATA	
berpikir	to think
bertindak	to act
lucu	funny

Summary

- Basic prepositions: **di**, **ke**, **dari**
- Compound prepositions: **di**, **ke** or **dari** + locative word (for example, **atas**, **bawah**)
- Other prepositions: **pada**, **kepada**, **selama**, **sampai**, **sebelum**, **sesudah**

6 Uses of *Ada*

The word **ada** can mean three different things, depending on the context.

- there is/are/was/were
- to be at a place
- to have

6.1 There is/are/was/were

Ada dua puluh orang murid di kelas ini.
There are twenty students in this class.

Di Jakarta ada banyak pertokoan besar.
In Jakarta there are many large shopping centres.

To say 'there isn't/aren't/wasn't/weren't', add the negative word **tidak** in front of **ada**.

Tidak ada ular di Selandia Baru kecuali di kebun binatang.
There are no snakes in New Zealand except in the zoo.

Tidak ada siapa-siapa di kantor itu.
There is no one in that office.

Handy expression
Ada berapa? means 'how many are/were there?'

Ada berapa komputer di ruangan ini?
How many computers are there in this room?

To ask 'What's the matter?', simply say **Ada apa?**

Ada apa? Kok menangis?
What's the matter? How come you're crying?

6.2 To be at a place

Bapak ada di garasi.
Father is in the garage.

Maaf, Ibu tidak ada di rumah.
Sorry, Mother is not home.

6.3 To have

Kamu ada uang?
Do you have (some) money?

Kasihan, dia tidak ada teman di sini.
Poor thing, he/she doesn't have any friends here.

LATIHAN 1

What is the meaning of **ada** in each of the sentences below?

1 Rini tidak ada di sekolah hari ini. Di mana dia?
2 Kami tidak ada mobil untuk pergi ke sana.
3 Teman saya Jerry sedang ada di Indonesia sekarang.
4 Ada banyak bebek di sekitar danau itu.
5 Sepatumu ada di lemari.
6 Apakah ada kantor pos di dekat sini?
7 Ada film bagus diputar di gedung bioskop.
8 Saya tidak ada uang untuk membeli tas baru.
9 Di kota itu ada berapa rumah sakit?
10 Anak Bu Ratna sekarang ada di Singapura.

KOSAKATA

bebek	duck
diputar	to be screened
sepatu	shoes
tas	bag

LATIHAN 2

Work in pairs for this exercise. Look at the following picture and take turns in using **ada** to ask questions about what you see. You may need to consult your dictionary for this exercise.

Example:

A: Ada apa di dinding?
What is there on the wall?
B: Di dinding ada jam.
On the wall there is a clock.

A: Di mana buku-buku?
Where are the books?
B: Buku-buku ada di rak.
The books are on the shelf.

Summary

- **Ada** can mean:
  —'there is/are/was/were'
  —'to be at a certain place'
  —in some cases, 'to have'
- To negate **ada**, add **tidak** in front of it.

1 Comparing

In this chapter we learn ways of comparing things:

- How to say 'more than' or 'less than' (comparative)
- How to say 'most' (superlative)
- How to say 'the same as' or 'as ... as' (equative)

Let us now look at each of these in turn.

1.1 How to say 'more than' or 'less than'

- **lebih ... dari(pada)**
- **kalah ... dibandingkan dengan**
- **kurang ...**

Lebih dari(pada)

One way to say 'more' in Indonesian is by using the word **lebih**.

LEBIH PHRASE	ENGLISH MEANING
lebih awal	earlier
lebih banyak	more (in quantity)
lebih biru	bluer
lebih cepat	quicker, faster
lebih kuning	yellower
lebih lama	longer
lebih lambat	slower
lebih mahal	more expensive
lebih murah	cheaper, less expensive
lebih pandai	cleverer, smarter

To say 'more than', **lebih** is followed by **dari** or **daripada**, which literally means 'from', but, when used for comparing, translates into English as 'than'.

Rumah saya lebih kecil dari(pada) rumah mereka.
My house is smaller than their house.

Anton lebih tinggi dari(pada) ayahnya.
Anton is taller than his father.

Handy expression

- If you want to give a polite answer to someone who, for example, asks you whether you have had enough to eat, you can say: **lebih dari cukup** (more than enough, sufficient).
- **Lebih** can be preceded by the word **jauh** (far) to emphasise a comparison.

Rumah saya jauh lebih kecil dari(pada) rumah mereka.
My house is far/much smaller than their house.

Anton jauh lebih tinggi dari(pada) ayahnya.
Anton is far/much taller than his father.

Kalah

Another way of comparing is by using **kalah**, which literally means 'to lose, be beaten', but, when used for comparing, means 'less'. To say 'less … than' in Indonesian, we would say **kalah … dibandingkan dengan**.

Australia kalah banyak penduduknya dibandingkan dengan India.
Australia has a smaller population than India.

Amin kalah tinggi dibandingkan dengan Rinto.
Amin is less tall than Rinto.

LATIHAN 1

Working in pairs, take turns to ask questions using **mana yang** (which one) + **lebih/kalah** for things, and **siapa yang** (who) + **lebih/kalah** for people.

Example:

A: Mana yang kalah besar: singa atau panda?
B: Panda.

You can vary the answer by saying **kedua-duanya** (both) if the things compared are similar (for example, in quality).

A: Mana yang lebih bagus: komputer IBM atau Macintosh?
B: Kedua-duanya.

1 Compare two car makes. Which is better?
2 Compare two kinds of fruit. Which is less sweet?
3 Compare the height of three of your friends. Who is taller than whom?
4 Compare the age of two people you know. Who is younger or older?
5 Compare two cities you know. Which is larger or nicer?
6 Compare chicken and beef. Which is less delicious?
7 Compare two modes of public transport, such as bus and tram. Which is less comfortable?
8 Compare two seasons in Australia, such as winter and summer. Which is more enjoyable?
9 Compare two tennis players. Who is slower (less fast)?
10 Compare two actors. Who is better?

KOSAKATA

bagus	nice
besar	large
cepat	fast
enak	delicious
enak, nyaman	comfortable
lambat, pelan	slow
manis	sweet
menyenangkan	enjoyable
muda	young
tinggi	tall
tua	old

Kurang

Kurang literally means 'not enough'.

KURANG PHRASE	ENGLISH MEANING
kurang banyak	not enough (quantity)
kurang cepat	not fast enough
kurang lama	not long enough
kurang panas	not hot enough

Kurang is not followed by **dari(pada)** in comparisons, since what the thing is compared to is not explicitly mentioned, even though we often have in our mind a standard for the comparison. For instance, if we say that the car is not going fast enough, we have in mind a certain speed that we are using for comparison.

Rambutnya kurang panjang.
His/her hair is not long enough.

Kopi ini kurang manis.
This coffee is not sweet enough.

Because the standard for comparison is not mentioned, we often hear people say, either in good humour or in annoyance, the following in response to the above statements:

Mau panjang seberapa?
How long do you think it should be?

Mau manis seperti apa?
How sweet do you want it to be?

When followed by **dari**, **kurang** means 'less than'.

KURANG DARI PHRASE	ENGLISH MEANING
kurang dari 50	less than 50
kurang dari setengahnya	less than half of it
kurang dari yang diharapkan	less than what is expected

Did you know?
Some people think that **kurang mahal** means 'less expensive', but in fact it means 'not expensive enough'. Be careful about using this phrase for bargaining in Indonesia, as you might inadvertently be asking for a higher price!

USING *KURANG* FOR POLITENESS

Interestingly, **kurang** can also mean 'not very, not too' when combined with certain adjectives. People often use it in this way when they wish to be polite and not say directly what they really think (since it may offend people). For example, rather than saying that something is bad, they might say 'not too good'. The real meaning of what they say may then be the opposite of the words used.

KURANG PHRASE	LITERAL ENGLISH MEANING	ENGLISH MEANING
kurang bagus	not very or not too good	bad
kurang hati-hati	not very or not too careful	clumsy, careless
kurang lengkap	not too complete or well stocked	incomplete, poorly stocked
kurang sehat	not very or not too healthy	ill
kurang sempurna	not very or not too perfect	imperfect

Handy expression
A common way of saying that you do not feel well is **kurang enak badan**, which literally means that your body does not feel too good (and not 'does not feel delicious', even though **enak** is also used for describing food!).

LATIHAN 2

Here are some questions about various things. Answer them by saying: **Saya kira kurang ...** (I think it is not very ...). You may need your dictionary to find some adjectives, or use those you have learnt so far.

KOSAKATA	
masakan	cooking, cuisine
pantai	beach
rasa	taste

Example:

Bagaimana film itu?
How was the film?
Saya kira kurang seru.
I think it was not exciting enough.

1. Bagaimana rasa masakan di restoran itu?
2. Bagaimana toko buku itu?
3. Bagaimana kebun binatang itu?
4. Bagaimana konser musik itu?
5. Bagaimana situasi ekonomi di negara itu?
6. Bagaimana kualitas barang itu?
7. Bagaimana tempat wisata itu?
8. Bagaimana kolam renang itu?
9. Bagaimana program televisi itu?
10. Bagaimana pantai itu?

7.2 How to say 'most'

- **paling**
- **ter-**

To say 'most' in Indonesian, we can use either the word **paling** or the prefix **ter-** (see also Chapter 14). This is called the *superlative*, which, in English, is also shown by the ending '-est'.

Siapa orang yang <u>paling</u> kaya di dunia?
Siapa orang yang <u>ter</u>kaya di dunia?

Who is the richest person in the world?

Apa kata yang paling panjang dalam bahasa Inggris?
Apa kata yang terpanjang dalam bahasa Inggris?
What is the longest word in English?

7.3 Saying 'same as' or 'as ... as'

- **se-**
- **sama ... (nya) dengan ...**

To say 'the same as ...' or 'as ... as' in Indonesian, we use either the prefix **se-** or the word **sama** (same). When **sama** is used, the adjective can be followed by **-nya** and then by **dengan** (with).

Jam tangan ini semahal jam tangan ibu saya.
Jam tangan ini sama mahal(nya) dengan jam tangan ibu saya.
This watch is as expensive as my mother's watch.

Kota kami sebesar kotamu.
Kota kami sama besarnya dengan kotamu.
Our town is as large as your town.

To say 'not the same as' or 'not as ... as', simply add **tidak** before **se-** or **sama**.

Dia tidak setinggi kamu.
He/she is not as tall as you.

Tasnya tidak sama besarnya dengan tasmu.
His/her bag is not as large as your bag.

LATIHAN 3

Choose a word from the box to complete each sentence. Each word may be used only once. You may need to consult your dictionary for this exercise.

KOSAKATA
gemuk fat
ramah friendly
ramai busy (with lots of people)

ramai	enak	jauh	ramah	gemuk
mewah	banyak	hijau	lengkap	arti

1 Satu liter adalah sama ____________nya dengan 1000 mililiter.
2 Kata 'pandai' sama ____________nya dengan 'clever' dalam bahasa Inggris.
3 Hotel kami tidak se ____________ hotel anda.
4 Warna daun ini tidak se ____________ daun itu.
5 Kota Malang di Jawa Timur tidak se ____________ kota Jakarta.
6 Guru kami sama ____________nya dengan guru kalian.
7 Dari sini, kantor pos sama ____________nya dengan bank.

8 Pusat pertokoan itu se ________________________ pusat pertokoan di dekat rumah saya.
9 Nasi goreng sama ________________________nya dengan gado-gado.
10 Ayam ini tidak se ________________________ ayammu.

LATIHAN 4

For each of the following groups, make up three sentences, using **lebih**, **kalah**, **paling/ter-** or **sama/se-** to compare the things in that group.

1	Darwin:	31 derajat Celcius	
	Sydney:	20 derajat Celcius	
	Melbourne:	18 derajat Celcius	
2	Harga per kg:	Pisang	Rp 10.000
		Mangga	Rp 15.000
		Rambutan	Rp 20.000
3	Setiap pagi:	Toni bangun jam 6	
		Ridwan bangun jam 6.30	
		Maria bangun jam 7	
4	Tebal buku:	Akutansi	200 halaman
		Bahasa Indonesia	230 halaman
		Sastra Inggris	310 halaman
5	Umur	Bu Endang	47 tahun
		Pak Made	35 tahun
		Bu Ratna	30 tahun
6	Undian	pertama ditarik	tanggal 20 Oktober
	Undian	kedua ditarik	tanggal 1 Nopember
	Undian	ketiga ditarik	tanggal 15 Desember

KOSAKATA

akutansi	accounting
ditarik	to be drawn (for raffles)
sastra Inggris	English literature
tebal	thickness
undian	lottery, raffle

Summary

Ways of comparing things:

- To say 'more than': use **lebih dari**
- To emphasise the comparison: use **jauh** in front of **lebih dari**
- To say 'much less than': use **kalah**
- To say 'not enough': use **kurang**
- To say 'most': use either **paling** or **ter-**
- To say 'same as' or 'as … as': use either **sama …(nya) dengan** or **se …**

8

Uses of *Yang*

Yang is very often used both in writing and speaking. It can mean 'the one' or 'which, who, whom', depending on the sentence.

> **Yang biru itu pena saya.**
> The blue one is my pen.
>
> **Lagu yang baru itu populer sekali.**
> The song which is new is very popular.
> → The new song is very popular.

More examples of the uses of **yang** are given below.

8.1 To refer to a person or thing

When used to refer to a person or thing, **yang** replaces the word for person (**orang**) or the word for the thing to which we are referring (for example, a pen). **Yang** in this case means 'the one'.

> **Yang berkacamata itu adalah kakak saya.**
> The one (person) who wears glasses is my older sibling.
>
> **Kamu boleh mengambil yang merah.**
> You can take the red one.

LATIHAN 1

Here are sentences with **yang** (the one). Find out what they mean in English. You may need to consult your dictionary for this exercise.

1. Saya mau yang merah.
2. Yang berdiri di sana itu namanya Daniel.
3. Kamu boleh meminjam yang plastik.
4. Yang tersenyum itu adalah bintang film terkenal.
5. Yang terlambat akan didenda.
6. Yang tebal itu adalah kamus Inggris-Indonesia.
7. Bis saya adalah yang nomer 87.
8. Buah rambutan adalah yang berwarna merah dan berambut.
9. Kunci kantor saya adalah yang nomer 258.
10. Film yang menang festival itu adalah yang dibintangi oleh Julia Roberts.

8.2 To say 'the person who(m) ...' or 'the thing that ...'

When used to say 'the person who(m) ...' or 'the thing that ...', **yang** is preceded by a noun.

Orang yang saya lihat di jalan kemarin itu adalah Bu Yani.
Noun *Who(m)*
The person whom I saw on the street yesterday was Bu Yani.

Email yang panjang itu adalah dari adiknya di Perancis.
Noun *Which*
Literally: The e-mail that is long was from his/her younger sibling in France.
→ That long e-mail was from his/her younger sibling in France.

LATIHAN 2

Complete the sentences in Indonesian with your own words.

Example:
Orang yang bekerja di kantor itu semua muda.

1 Foto yang ...
2 Restoran yang ...
3 Pesan yang ...
4 Kopi yang ...
5 Olahraga yang ...
6 Kota yang ...
7 Surat yang ...
8 Penerbangan yang ...
9 Alat musik yang ...
10 Binatang yang ...

KOSAKATA

alat musik	musical instrument
penerbangan	flight
pesan	message

8.3 Asking 'which (one)?'

To ask 'which?' or 'which one?' we can say **yang mana?**

Rumahmu yang mana?

Or:

Yang mana rumahmu?
Which one is your house?

Yang hijau.
The green one.

Mau pakai baju yang mana?
Which shirt do you want to wear?

Yang putih.
The white one.

LATIHAN 3

Work in pairs for this exercise. Below are five questions with **Yang mana bukan ...?** (Which one is not ...?). Provide a choice of five answers to each question, then ask your friend to choose the correct answer.

Example:

Yang mana bukan nama anggota tubuh?
Which one is not the name of a body part?

a **mata**
b **kelapa**
c **perut**
d **mulut**
e **punggung**

Answer: **kelapa** (coconut)

1 Yang mana bukan nama orang laki-laki?
2 Yang mana bukan binatang berekor?
3 Yang mana bukan nama jenis anjing?
4 Yang mana bukan nama makanan?
5 Yang mana bukan nama alat musik?

Summary

- **Yang** can mean 'the one', replacing the word for a person or thing.
- **Yang** can also be used to mean 'who(m)' or 'which' in the sense of 'the person who(m) ...' or 'the thing which ...'.
- **Yang mana**: is used to ask questions meaning 'which one'.

9

Transitive and Intransitive Verbs

Traditionally, a *verb* is defined as a 'doing word' or 'action word'. While this definition may be applicable to many verbs, it is inaccurate for some others, because verbs can also refer to states or conditions. The verb **berhenti** (stop) in Indonesian, for example, means 'to be in a stationary position', so there is no action as such.

In Indonesian, we need to distinguish between *intransitive* and *transitive* verbs, according to whether the verb requires only one or more than one noun to accompany it to make sense when we use it in a sentence.

9.1 Intransitive verbs

An *intransitive verb* is a verb that needs only one noun (or noun phrase) to accompany it in a sentence. We refer to this noun (phrase) as the *subject*. **Duduk** (sit) and **berlari** (run) are examples of intransitive verbs.

SUBJECT	INTRANSITIVE VERB
Anto	**duduk.**
Anto	sits.
Nenek	**berjalan.**
Grandmother	walks.
Adik saya	**menangis.**
My younger sibling	cries.

In a sentence you can add something other than a noun after the intransitive verb, such as a *prepositional phrase* (a preposition followed by a noun) or a *manner adverb* (a word placed after a verb that tells us the manner in which an action is done).

SUBJECT	INTRANSITIVE VERB	PREPOSITIONAL PHRASE
Anto	**duduk**	**di kursi.**
Anto	sits	on the chair.
Nenek	**berjalan**	**ke pasar.**
Grandmother	walks	to market.

SUBJECT	INTRANSITIVE VERB	MANNER ADVERB
Ani	**menangis**	**keras.**
Ani	cries	loudly.
Tono	**tidur**	**lelap.**
Tono	sleeps	soundly.

We can also make the sentences more complex by combining a manner adverb with a prepositional phrase.

SUBJECT	INTRANSITIVE VERB	MANNER ADVERB	PREPOSITIONAL PHRASE
Tono	**tidur**	**lelap**	**di kursi.**
Tono	sleeps	soundly	on the chair.
Nenek	**berjalan**	**cepat**	**ke pasar.**
Grandmother	walks	quickly	to market.

Intransitive verbs take different forms. Some have no affix, some have the **ber-** prefix, some have the **meN-** prefix and some have the **ter-** prefix. The tables below list only some of the intransitive verbs in each of these groups. The capital letter **N** in the prefix **meN-** indicates the sound change that occurs when the prefix is attached to a base word (see Chapter 11).

Simple intransitive verbs (no affix)

INTRANSITIVE VERB	ENGLISH MEANING
datang	to come
duduk	to sit
hidup	to live
ingat	to remember
jatuh	to fall
keluar	to exit, go out of
lulus	to pass (an exam) or test
lupa	to forget
mandi	to bathe oneself
masuk	to enter, go into
mulai	to start, begin
percaya	to believe
pergi	to go
pindah	to move from one place to another

INTRANSITIVE VERB	ENGLISH MEANING
pulang	to go home
selesai	to finish
singgah	to stop over
tahu	to know
terbang	to fly
tiba	to arrive
tidur	to sleep
tinggal	to stay, live (reside)

Intransitive verbs with *ber-*

(For other examples, see Chapter 10.)

BASE WORD	INTRANSITIVE VERB	ENGLISH MEANING
ajar	**belajar**	to learn, study
angkat	**berangkat**	to leave, depart
bahasa	**berbahasa**	to use a language
baring	**berbaring**	to lie down
belanja	**berbelanja**	to go shopping
bicara	**berbicara**	to speak
buat	**berbuat**	to do, commit
cakap	**bercakap**	to chat
diri	**berdiri**	to stand
gurau	**bergurau**	to joke around
hati	**berhati-hati**	to take care
henti	**berhenti**	to stop (be stationary)
hias	**berhias**	to groom oneself
istirahat	**beristirahat**	to take a rest
jalan	**berjalan**	to walk
kembang	**berkembang**	to develop
kerja	**bekerja**	to work
kuasa	**berkuasa**	to have the authority
kumpul	**berkumpul**	to gather
lari	**berlari**	to run
libur	**berlibur**	to go on a holiday
main	**bermain**	to play
nyanyi	**bernyanyi**	to sing
pegang	**berpegang**	to hold on to
perang	**berperang**	to engage in a war
renang	**berenang**	to swim
selancar	**berselancar**	to surf
sembahyang	**bersembahyang**	to pray
tandang	**bertandang**	to visit someone
temu	**bertemu**	to meet
ubah	**berubah**	to change

Note
In the verbs **belajar**, **berenang** and **bekerja** the '**r**' in the prefix **ber-** is dropped. In **bekerja** and **berenang** it is dropped altogether, whereas in **belajar** it is replaced by '**l**'.

Intransitive verbs with *meN-*

BASE WORD	INTRANSITIVE VERB	ENGLISH MEANING
bual	**membual**	to boast
cangkul	**mencangkul**	to hoe
dengkur	**mendengkur**	to snore
inap	**menginap**	to stay the night
lompat	**melompat**	to jump
nyanyi	**menyanyi**	to sing
rangkak	**merangkak**	to crawl
rokok	**merokok**	to smoke
tangis	**menangis**	to cry
tari	**menari**	to dance
tinggal	**meninggal**	to die
uap	**menguap**	to yawn

Intransitive verbs with *ter-*

BASE WORD	INTRANSITIVE VERB	ENGLISH MEANING
senyum	**tersenyum**	to smile
tawa	**tertawa**	to laugh

LATIHAN 1

Write a caption in Indonesian for each of the following pictures using the intransitive verbs listed in the preceding tables.

Note

Some intransitive verbs can take either the **ber-** or the **meN-** prefix with no difference in meaning.

bernyanyi/menyanyi	to sing
berbekas/membekas	to leave a mark or trace

Some other intransitive verbs take what are sometimes called *pseudo-objects* (nouns that look like objects, but are not perceived as being affected by the action)—see section 9.2.

bermain gitar	to play the guitar
bertepuk tangan	to clap (one's) hands
bersepatu roda	to roller-skate

In these cases, we treat the verb and the following word as constituting one activity. In the previous examples, the words **gitar**, **tangan** and **roda** are considered as part of the verbs **bermain**, **bertepuk** and **bersepatu** respectively.

9.2 Transitive verbs

A *transitive* verb requires more than one noun or noun phrase for it to occur in a sentence. One of the nouns or noun phrases serves as the subject (as in intransitive verbs), while the other noun or noun phrase serves as *object*. Because the subject is typically the instigator of an action, we also refer to it as the *actor*. The object, on the other hand, is the person or thing that is affected by that action. We also refer to it as the *patient*.

SUBJECT (ACTOR)	TRANSITIVE VERB	OBJECT (PATIENT)
Kakak	**membaca**	**surat.**
Older sibling	reads	the letter.
Ibu	**membawa**	**keranjang.**
Mother	carries	the basket.
Pak Harun	**membuka**	**pintu.**
Mr Harun	opens	the door.

Many transitive verbs have the **meN-** prefix.

BASE WORD	TRANSITIVE VERB	ENGLISH MEANING
ajak	**mengajak**	to invite someone to do something
ajar	**mengajar**	to teach
angkat	**mengangkat**	to lift
antar	**mengantar**	to take someone/something somewhere
atur	**mengatur**	to arrange, organise
baca	**membaca**	to read
bahas	**membahas**	to discuss
bakar	**membakar**	to burn
bantah	**membantah**	to deny
bawa	**membawa**	to carry
bayar	**membayar**	to pay
bela	**membela**	to defend
beri	**memberi**	to give
beritahu	**memberitahu**	to inform
buka	**membuka**	to open
cari	**mencari**	to search, look for
cuci	**mencuci**	to wash
culik	**menculik**	to kidnap
curi	**mencuri**	to steal
daki	**mendaki**	to climb (a mountain)
dapat	**mendapat**	to get, obtain, gain
dukung	**mendukung**	to support
gali	**menggali**	to dig
ganggu	**mengganggu**	to disturb
ganti	**mengganti**	to replace
hias	**menghias**	to decorate
intip	**mengintip**	to peep
isi	**mengisi**	to fill
jaga	**menjaga**	to take care
jahit	**menjahit**	to sew
jawab	**menjawab**	to reply
jemput	**menjemput**	to pick someone up
jual	**menjual**	to sell
lihat	**melihat**	to see, look
masak	**memasak**	to cook
mulai	**memulai**	to begin
pakai	**memakai**	to wear, use
panggil	**memanggil**	to call, summon
panjat	**memanjat**	to climb (a tree)

BASE WORD	TRANSITIVE VERB	ENGLISH MEANING
pasang	**memasang**	to set up, install
periksa	**memeriksa**	to check, inspect
pesan	**memesan**	to order
pilih	**memilih**	to choose
pinang	**meminang**	to propose (marriage)
pinta	**meminta**	to ask for something, request
rusak	**merusak**	to damage intentionally
salin	**menyalin**	to copy
sapu	**menyapu**	to sweep (floor, yard)
sewa	**menyewa**	to rent
simpan	**menyimpan**	to store, keep
siram	**menyiram**	to water, spray
tangkap	**menangkap**	to catch
tarik	**menarik**	to pull
tawar	**menawar**	to bargain
telpon	**menelpon**	to telephone
tonton	**menonton**	to watch
tunggu	**menunggu**	to wait
tunjuk	**menunjuk**	to point, choose
tutup	**menutup**	to close
ulang	**mengulang**	to repeat
undang	**mengundang**	to invite (for example, to a party)
urus	**mengurus**	to organise

Note

Many of the transitive verbs listed in the table above can also function as intransitive verbs when they are used without an object. **Memberi** (to give) is a good example.

Intransitive:

> **Dia suka memberi.**
> He/she likes giving.

Transitive:

> **Dia suka memberi uang.**
> He/she likes giving out money.

LATIHAN 2

The following pictures illustrate people doing things. Write a caption in Indonesian for each picture using a transitive verb.

9.3 Deriving transitive from the intransitive

As we have seen, what distinguishes an intransitive verb from a transitive verb is primarily the number of noun or noun phrases that occur with it in a sentence. Often, however, we find that an intransitive verb can be transformed into a transitive verb using certain mechanisms. Ways in which we can do this are discussed below.

Adding an object

The verb **membaca** (to read) can be used as an intransitive verb or as a transitive verb without changing its form. It is the addition of an object that makes it transitive.

SUBJECT	INTRANSITIVE VERB
Mereka They	**membaca.** read.
Ibu Mother	**makan.** eats.

SUBJECT	TRANSITIVE VERB	OBJECT
Mereka	**membaca**	**buku.**
They	read	a book.
Ibu	**makan**	**bakmi goreng.**
Mother	eats	fried noodles.

Adding the suffix *-kan* or *-i*

Some intransitive verbs can be transformed into transitive verbs by either changing the affixation from **ber-** to **meN–kan** or **meN–i** or by adding some affixes when there are none. When we do this, the meaning of the verbs sometimes stays the same and sometimes changes.

SUBJECT	INTRANSITIVE VERB	PREPOSITIONAL PHRASE
Dia	**berbicara**	**di kelas.**
He/she	talks	in class.
Mira	**bertemu**	**dengan dia.**
Mira	meets	with him/her.

SUBJECT	TRANSITIVE VERB	OBJECT	PREPOSITIONAL PHRASE
Dia	**membicarakan**	**hal itu**	**di kelas.**
He/she	talks about (discusses)	that matter	in class.
Ali	**menemui**	**saya**	**di rumah.**
Ali	came to see	me	at home.

Note

Here is how you can tell whether the verb in a sentence is transitive or intransitive. Intransitive verbs can be followed directly by a preposition (such as **di** or **dengan**). Transitive verbs must be followed directly by an object; there cannot be a preposition intercepting between the verb and the object.

Notice the transformation below from intransitive (verb + preposition) to transitive (verb with **meN-** prefix and either suffix **-kan** or **-i**).

Intransitive: Rita <u>**cinta kepada**</u> Faisal.
Rita <u>loves</u> Faisal. (Literally 'loves to')

Transitive: Rita <u>**mencintai**</u> Faisal.
Rita <u>loves</u> Faisal.

Intransitive: **Saya <u>suka akan</u> film itu.**
I <u>like</u> that film. (Literally 'like at')

Transitive: **Saya <u>menyukai</u> film itu.**
I <u>like</u> that film.

Intransitive: **Andi <u>marah kepada</u> temannya.**
Andi <u>is angry with</u> his friend.

Transitive:	**Andi memarahi temannya.** Andi scolded his friend.
Intransitive:	**Mereka berkumpul di aula.** They gathered in the hall.
Transitive:	**Guru mengumpulkan murid-murid di aula.** The teacher gathered the students in the hall.

LATIHAN 3

The pictures below illustrate people doing something. Write a caption in Indonesian for each picture using an intransitive verb. Next, rewrite the captions, transforming each intransitive verb into a transitive verb by adding an object.

LATIHAN 4

The following verbs are from the tables of transitive and intransitive verbs that you saw earlier in this chapter. Copy and complete the following table to make sentences. The left-hand column is for the subject of the sentence, while the other columns are for the object (if there is one), the prepositional phrase (indicating location) and for any other information that you wish to add to the sentence.

	SUBJECT	VERB	OBJECT	PREPOSITIONAL PHRASE	OTHER INFORMATION
1		makan			
2		membaca			
3		menjahit			
4		pindah			
5		berlibur			
6		mencuri			
7		berbelanja			
8		menjemput			
9		menyewa			
10		membela			

LATIHAN 5

Work in pairs to do this exercise.

- Person A: Act out five verbs from the verb tables in this chapter and ask your friend: **Saya sedang apa?** (What am I doing?)
- Person B: Answer the question in a sentence beginning with: **Kamu sedang …** (You are …)

You need to identify whether the verb required is intransitive or transitive. If the verb is intransitive, you can add a prepositional phrase or something else. If the verb is transitive, you need to add an object, followed by some other information if you wish.

Examples:

A: Saya sedang apa?
B: Kamu sedang merokok.

A: Saya sedang apa?
B: Kamu sedang tidur di meja.

Take turns in asking and answering questions.

Summary

- Intransitive verbs take a subject but no object → [Subject – Verb].
- Transitive verbs take a subject and an object → [Subject – Verb – Object].
- Forms of intransitive verbs: affix-less, [**ber-** + base word], [**meN-** + base word].
- Forms of transitive verbs: [**meN-** + base word], [**meN-** + **-kan**], [**meN-** + **-i**].
- Only intransitive verbs can be followed directly by a preposition, such as **di**, **ke**, **dengan** or **akan**. Transitive verbs have to be followed directly by an object.

10

Ber-

Ber- is often called a verbal prefix. This is because most of the words with this prefix are verbs, even though they may be derived from nouns, verbs or other sources. We saw in Chapter 9 that **ber-** verbs are intransitive; that is, they occur with only one noun (or noun phrase) in a sentence and this noun is the subject of the sentence.

In this chapter we look at the different meanings of **ber-** words:

- **Ber-** verbs and not verbs
- **Ber–an**

10.1 To have what the base word indicates

Ber- in this group roughly means 'to have'. However, when we translate it into English, we may use the ending '-ed', or use 'of' or 'have'.

berkaki empat	four-legged
berumur lima tahun	be five years of age
berkumis	have a moustache

BASE WORD	ENGLISH MEANING	BER- WORD	ENGLISH MEANING
anak	child	**beranak**	to have a child
jenggot	beard	**berjenggot**	to have a beard
kaki	foot	**berkaki**	to have feet
kulit	skin	**berkulit**	to have skin
kumis	moustache	**berkumis**	to have a moustache
nama	name	**bernama**	to have the name (be called)
rambut	hair	**berambut**	to have hair
uang	money	**beruang**	to have money (be wealthy)
umur	age	**berumur**	to have age (be a certain age)

Did you know?
The word **beruang** can mean three different things, depending on the base word from which it is derived.

BASE WORD	ENGLISH MEANING	BER- WORD	ENGLISH MEANING
uang	money	**ber + uang**	to have money (be wealthy)
ruang	room	**be(r) + ruang**	to have room (house, building)
beruang	bear (animal)	**beruang**	bear (the animal)

10.2 To use or wear

This group includes words pertaining to things we wear (items of clothing) or use (including some vehicles, such as cars and bikes).

BASE WORD	ENGLISH MEANING	BER- VERB	ENGLISH MEANING
baju	shirt, attire	**berbaju**	to wear (attire)
jins	jeans	**berjins**	to wear jeans
kacamata	glasses	**berkacamata**	to wear glasses
mobil	car	**bermobil**	to go by car
sepatu	shoe	**bersepatu**	to wear shoes
sepeda	bicycle	**bersepeda**	to go by bicycle
sepeda motor	motorbike	**bersepeda motor**	to go by motorbike
singlet	singlet	**bersinglet**	to wear a singlet
tongkat	walking stick	**bertongkat**	to use a walking stick
topi	hat	**bertopi**	to wear a hat

LATIHAN 1

Complete the following sentences with **ber-** words.

1 Benarkah bahwa orang Indonesia ______________________ coklat?
2 Ibu saya ______________________ 41 tahun.
3 Kami ______________________ ke Canberra.
4 Mereka keluarga yang ______________________ Rumah mereka besar sekali dan mobil mereka mewah.
5 Lina sangat suka ______________________ Levi's ke mana-mana.

KOSAKATA
mewah luxurious, very expensive

LATIHAN 2

Write a short caption in Indonesian for each of the following pictures using **ber-** words. You may need to consult your dictionary for this exercise.

10.3 To do what the base word indicates

The following verbs represent only a few of the **ber-** verbs. For more examples, refer to Chapter 9.

BASE WORD	ENGLISH MEANING	**BER-** VERB	ENGLISH MEANING
cerita	story	**bercerita**	to tell a story
cermin	mirror	**bercermin**	to look at oneself in the mirror
gerak	motion	**bergerak**	to move
latih	exercise, train	**berlatih**	to train (physical exercise), to do exercise (not physical, such as music, maths)
libur	holiday	**berlibur**	to take a vacation
perang	war	**berperang**	to engage in a war
siul	whistle	**bersiul**	to whistle
tambah	add, increase	**bertambah**	to increase
tandang	visit	**bertandang**	to visit
temu	meet	**bertemu**	to meet
tugas	task, duty	**bertugas**	to have a task/duty

Note

Formal and informal forms

Sometimes words with the **ber-** prefix have the same meaning as those that do not have the **ber-** prefix. When speaking, Indonesians use either word. Words with the **ber-** prefix are more formal and this is the correct form to use when you write in Indonesian.

BASE WORD	ENGLISH MEANING	**BER**- VERB	ENGLISH MEANING
belanja	to shop	**berbelanja**	to shop
dagang	to do business, sell	**berdagang**	to do business, sell
kumpul	to gather	**berkumpul**	to gather
main	to play	**bermain**	to play
nyanyi	to sing	**bernyanyi**	to sing

Spelling
When attached to certain base words, the 'r' in **ber-** is either replaced by another letter or, if the base word begins with 'r', it is dropped altogether. Throughout the rest of this chapter, an asterisk (*) is used to indicate words to which the spelling change applies.

BASE WORD	ENGLISH MEANING	**BER**- VERB	ENGLISH MEANING
ajar	to teach	***belajar**	to learn, study
kerja	to work	***bekerja**	to work
renang	to swim	***berenang**	to swim
runding	to negotiate	***berunding**	to negotiate

10.4 *Ber- + numeral*

When attached to a numeral, **ber-** means 'in + number'.

BASE WORD	ENGLISH MEANING	**BER**- WORD	ENGLISH MEANING
lima	five	**berlima**	group of five people (Literally: in five)
dua	two	**berdua**	two people together (Literally: in two)

However, note the following.

BASE WORD	ENGLISH MEANING	**BER**- VERB	ENGLISH MEANING
satu	one	**bersatu**	to unite (to be one)

10.5 *Ber–an*

When the suffix **-an** is attached to a **ber-** verb, the verb will indicate either 'reciprocality' or 'irregularity of action or motion'.

Reciprocality

'Reciprocality' means that the verbs indicate mutual action or relationship between two or more people, animals or inanimate objects (for example, vehicles).

BASE WORD	ENGLISH MEANING	BER- VERB	ENGLISH MEANING
bentur	to knock, hit	**berbenturan**	to knock or hit each other
cium	to kiss	**berciuman**	to be kissing (two people)
dekat	near	**berdekatan**	to be in close proximity to each other
dua	two	**berduaan**	to be alone with a partner (Literally: in two)
hadap	face	**berhadapan**	to face each other
jabat	to shake hand	**berjabatan (tangan)**	to shake hands
jauh	far	**berjauhan**	to be distant from each other
kenal	to know	**berkenalan**	to introduce oneself to someone
musuh	enemy	**bermusuhan**	to be each other's enemy
pandang	gaze, look	**berpandangan**	to gaze/look at each other
papas	to come across	**berpapasan**	to meet or bump into someone
pegang	to hold	**berpegangan (tangan)**	to hold hands
sebelah	side	**bersebelahan**	to be side by side
seberang	across	**berseberangan**	to be across from each other
tabrak	to hit, collide	**bertabrakan**	to collide

Irregular action or motion

BASE WORD	ENGLISH MEANING	BER- VERB	ENGLISH MEANING
datang	to come	**berdatangan**	to arrive one after another
kejar	to chase	**berkejaran**	to chase each other
lari	to run	**berlarian**	to run everywhere (to and fro)
tebar	to scatter	**bertebaran**	to be scattered
terbang	to fly	***beterbangan**	to fly everywhere

Waktu berkenalan, orang Indonesia biasanya berjabatan tangan.
When introducing themselves, Indonesians usually shake hands.

Mobil itu bertabrakan dengan truk.
That car collided with a truck.

Tamu-tamu mulai berdatangan ke pesta itu.
Guests are starting to arrive at that party.

LATIHAN 3

Working in pairs, choose one of the following sentences to act out in front of the class. The other students in the class have to guess what you are doing without looking at the **ber–an** verbs on the previous page. Include some conversation, if need be, to enable the class to guess, rather than just miming.

1 Anda berdua berdiri **berseberangan** kemudian **berpandangan.**
2 Anda berdua duduk **berjauhan** di kelas karena anda **bermusuhan.**
3 Anda berdua baru **berkenalan**, dan setelah berbicara beberapa menit, anda mengetahui bahwa ternyata anda **bertetangga**.
4 Ketika mobil dan sepeda motor anda **bertabrakan**, orang-orang **berdatangan** untuk melihat apa yang terjadi.
5 Anda berdua **berpapasan** di jalan, lalu **berjabatan tangan** karena sudah lama tidak bertemu.

10.6 Reduplicated *ber-*

When **ber-** is reduplicated, the word may indicate repeated or extended action, or action that takes place over an extended period of time. Reduplicated **ber-** may also indicate plural.

Repeated or extended action, or action over an extended time

REDUPLICATED **BER**- WORD	ENGLISH MEANING
berbincang-bincang	to talk, discuss
bercakap-cakap	to talk, chat
berjalan-jalan	to walk at leisure, stroll
berjingkrak-jingkrak	to jump up and down in excitement
berputar-putar	to go round and round

Handy expression

A useful common expression is **berlama-lama** (purposely take time in doing something).

Jangan berlama-lama di sana ya.
Don't stay too long there, will you?

Lisa berlama-lama mandi karena airnya hangat.
Lisa is taking her time showering since the water is warm.

Plural

REDUPLICATED **BER-** WORD	ENGLISH MEANING
berbeda-beda	different kinds
bermacam-macam	various kinds
***beratus-ratus**	hundreds of
***beribu-ribu**	thousands of

LATIHAN 4

Describe one of the following animals in Indonesian using **ber-** verbs. You should describe the animal's skin colour, eyes, mouth, teeth, whether it is two-legged or four-legged and so on. The other students in the class have to guess what animal it is.

1 **burung flamingo** (flamingo)
2 **ikan hiu** (shark)
3 **kodok/katak** (frog)
4 **kuda nil** (hippopotamus)
5 **kuda zebra** (zebra)
6 **kura-kura** (turtle)

LATIHAN 5

On 28 October 1928, during the Youth Congress, the Indonesian Youth made a pledge that became known as **Sumpah Pemuda** (Youth Pledge). This pledge is a formal declaration of the existence of the Indonesian nation and the adoption of a national language (originally Malay). **Hari Sumpah Pemuda** (Youth Pledge Day) is annually commemorated on 28 October as a remembrance of this occasion.

Translate the pledge into English.

> **Sumpah Pemuda**
> Kami, putra-putri Indonesia mengaku:
> Bertanah air satu, Tanah Air Indonesia
> Berbangsa satu, Bangsa Indonesia
> Berbahasa satu, Bahasa Indonesia

Summary

- **Ber-** can mean to have, to use or wear, or to do what the base word indicates.
- **Ber-** + numeral means 'in + number'.
- **Ber–an** indicates reciprocality or irregularity of action or motion.
- Reduplicated **ber-** indicates repeated action or action over an extended time, or plural.

11

MeN-

In this chapter we will learn more about **meN-** words, which can be verbs or adjectives.

We saw in Chapter 9 that **meN-** verbs can be either transitive (with an object following the verb) or intransitive (with no object following the verb).

Transitive:

Mereka	**membeli**	**pakaian**	**di toko murah itu.**
Subject	*Verb*	*Object*	*Prepositional phrase*
They	bought	clothes	in that cheap shop.

Intransitive:

Anita	**menyanyi**	**di kamar mandi.**
Subject	*Verb*	*Prepositional phrase*
Anita	sang	in the bathroom.

11.1 Sound changes

When we affix **meN-** to a base word, often a sound change occurs; that is, the sound of the initial letter of the base word is changed. If the base word begins with certain letters, there is no change. The capital letter **N** in **meN-** is used to indicate this change.

INITIAL LETTER OF BASE WORD	EXAMPLE OF BASE WORD	PREFIX	EXAMPLE OF **MEN-** VERB	ENGLISH MEANING
l	**lihat**	**me-**	**melihat**	to see, look
m	**maki**		**memaki**	to swear
n	**nanti**		**menanti**	to wait
ng	**nganga**		**menganga**	to be agape
ny	**nyanyi**		**menyanyi**	to sing
r	**raba**		**meraba**	to touch, feel
y	**yakin**		**meyakinkan**	to convince
w	**warna**		**mewarnai**	to colour

INITIAL LETTER OF BASE WORD	EXAMPLE OF BASE WORD	PREFIX	EXAMPLE OF **MEN-** VERB	ENGLISH MEANING
b	**bisu**	**mem-**	**membisu**	to stay mute
f	**fitnah**		**memfitnah**	to slander
v	**vonis**		**memvonis**	to sentence
*p	**pukul**		**memukul**	to hit
d	**dengkur**	**men-**	**mendengkur**	to snore
j	**jajah**		**menjajah**	to colonise
c	**cari**		**mencari**	to look for
*t	**tari**		**menari**	to dance
a	**atur**	**meng-**	**mengatur**	to organise
e	**erang**		**mengerang**	to moan
i	**ikat**		**mengikat**	to tie
o	**obrol**		**mengobrol**	to chat
u	**ukur**		**mengukur**	to measure
g	**garuk**		**menggaruk**	to scratch
h	**hukum**		**menghukum**	to punish
*k	**kejar**		**mengejar**	to chase
*s	**setir**	**meny-**	**menyetir**	to drive

Note
Initial sounds indicated by an asterisk (*) in the above are dropped when prefixed by **meN-**.

LATIHAN 1

Form **meN-** words by applying the above rules to each of the following base words. Then find the meaning in English of each **meN-** word by consulting your dictionary.

BASE WORD	*MEN-* WORD	ENGLISH MEANING
1 kira		
2 masak		
3 potong		
4 rusak		
5 buka		
6 gambar		
7 tulis		
8 bawa		
9 sesal		
10 hafal		
11 gapai		
12 lotot		

BASE WORD	*MEN-* WORD	ENGLISH MEANING
13 kepit		
14 umpat		
15 ambil		
16 ekor		
17 nebeng		
18 cium		
19 tolak		
20 usap		

LATIHAN 2

Working in pairs, take turns to do the following.

1. Practise pronouncing the base words and the **meN-** words from Latihan 1.
2. Act out each of the verbs while your partner guesses the meaning.

11.2 Transitive *meN-* verbs

In transitive verbs, **meN-** indicates *active voice* (also called *subject-focus*). That is, it tells us that the focus of the sentence is on the actor, who is also the subject of the sentence.

MeN- contrasts with the **di-** prefix in that **di-** indicates *passive voice* (also called *object-focus*), where the focus is on the object of the sentence. This contrast is discussed in more detail in Chapter 19.

MeN- verbs with noun base

Some transitive **meN-** verbs come from nouns. The following verbs mean 'do something associated with the base word' or 'using what is indicated by the base word'.

BASE WORD	ENGLISH MEANING	**MEN-** VERB	ENGLISH MEANING
borgol	handcuff	**memborgol**	to handcuff
cat	paint	**mencat, mengecat**	to paint (for example, the wall)
parut	grater	**memarut**	to grate
sapu	broom	**menyapu**	to sweep (for example, shoes, hair, but not furniture)
semir	polish	**menyemir**	to polish
sisir	comb	**menyisir**	to comb

MeN- verbs with verbal base

Other **meN-** verbs have a verbal base and, as mentioned in Chapter 10, the presence of the prefix is required to make a well-formed verb.

BASE WORD	ENGLISH MEANING	MEN- VERB	ENGLISH MEANING
baca	to read	**membaca**	to read
buka	to open	**membuka**	to open
lihat	to look, see	**melihat**	to look, see
siram	to spray, water	**menyiram**	to spray, water (for example, the garden)
tutup	to close, shut	**menutup**	to close, shut

11.3 Intransitive *meN-* verbs

With intransitive verbs, the prefix **meN-** indicates different meanings.

Formation of base word

As with transitive verbs, the **meN**- prefix is needed in some intransitive verbs for the base word to be well formed or make sense. In some cases, the base word cannot occur without it.

BASE WORD	MEN- VERB	ENGLISH MEANING
didih	**mendidih**	to boil
erti	**mengerti**	to understand
inap	**menginap**	to stay the night (for example, at a friend's house or at a hotel)
ungsi	**mengungsi**	to flee (for example, as refugees)

To do something associated with the base word

BASE WORD	ENGLISH MEANING	MEN- VERB	ENGLISH MEANING
ludah	spit	**meludah**	to spit
rokok	cigarette	**merokok**	to smoke
susu	milk	**menyusu**	to suckle

To be like what the base word indicates

BASE WORD	ENGLISH MEANING	MEN- VERB	ENGLISH MEANING
gunung	mountain	**menggunung**	to pile up
puncak	peak	**memuncak**	to peak, culminate

To go to where the base word indicates

BASE WORD	ENGLISH MEANING	MEN- VERB	ENGLISH MEANING
darat	land	**mendarat**	to go to land, to land
dekat	near	**mendekat**	to move close
jauh	far	**menjauh**	to move away
seberang	across	**menyeberang**	to go to the other side, to cross

Sound words (onomatopoeia)

These are words that resemble the noise made by either animals or humans.

BASE WORD	ENGLISH MEANING	MEN-VERB	ENGLISH MEANING
aum	roar	**mengaum**	to roar (for example, tigers)
cicit	squeak	**mencicit**	to squeak (for example, mice)
dengkur	snore	**mendengkur**	to snore
embik	bleat	**mengembik**	to bleat
eong	miaow	**mengeong**	to miaow
gonggong	bark	**menggonggong**	to bark
keluh	sigh	**mengeluh**	to sigh, complain
raung	roar, wail	**meraung**	to roar, wail
ringkik	neigh	**meringkik**	to neigh

To become what the base word indicates

BASE WORD	ENGLISH MEANING	MEN- VERB	ENGLISH MEANING
bengkak	swollen	**membengkak**	to swell
busuk	rotten	**membusuk**	to rot, go off (for example, food)
cair	liquid	**mencair**	to melt
kering	dry	**mengering**	to dry up
kuning	yellow	**menguning**	to become yellow → ripen (for example, rice plants)
putih	white	**memutih**	to become white → greying (for example, hair)
tebal	thick	**menebal**	to thicken
tipis	thin	**menipis**	to thin out

Some words having this meaning can also be used in a metaphorical sense.

BASE WORD	ENGLISH MEANING	MEN- VERB	ENGLISH MEANING
runcing	pointy	**meruncing**	to become pointy → become heated or acute (for example, conflict or argument)

11.4 *MeN-* adjectives

Interestingly, some **meN-** words are adjectives rather than verbs. For example, the following **meN-** words mean 'in the shape indicated by the base word'.

BASE WORD	ENGLISH MEANING	MEN- ADJECTIVE	ENGLISH MEANING
lingkar	circle	**melingkar**	curled
panjang	long	**memanjang**	lengthwise, elongated

Another example is the word **menarik**, which comes from the verb **tarik** (pull). The meaning of the adjective **menarik** is derived from the metaphorical sense of 'pull'; something that pulls or attracts your attention is something interesting or attractive.

menarik (verb)	to pull
menarik (adjective)	interesting, attractive

11.5 Undifferentiated *meN-* and *ber-* verbs

In very few cases, **meN-** verbs mean the same as their corresponding **ber-** verbs.

MEN- VERB	BER- VERB	ENGLISH MEANING
membekas	**berbekas**	to leave a mark or trace
menyanyi	**bernyanyi**	to sing

LATIHAN 3

KOSAKATA

danau	lake
darah	blood
dinding	wall
mendapatkan	to get, obtain
tetangga	neighbour

Indicate whether the following sentences are transitive or intransitive. The verbs to which you should pay attention are underlined.

1 Polisi <u>memborgol</u> tangan pencuri itu.
2 Bibi saya <u>mengeluh</u> tentang suaminya setiap hari.
3 Anjing tetangga saya selalu <u>menggonggong</u> pada malam hari.
4 Kami membantu <u>memarut</u> kelapa di dapur.
5 Pada musim panas danau itu <u>mengering</u>.

6 Presiden itu menginap di hotel bintang lima.
7 Darahnya mendidih ketika mendengar berita itu.
8 Ketika melihat saya dia menjauh.
9 Kakak saya mencat dinding kamarnya kemarin.
10 Mereka menyemir sepatu untuk mendapatkan uang.

LATIHAN 4

Write the following sentences in Indonesian. You will find the underlined words in this chapter. You may need to consult your dictionary for this exercise.

1 The snake curled up on the tree.
2 My mother's story is very interesting.
3 The food is starting to go off.
4 My father's hair is greying.
5 Goats and sheep bleat.
6 My friend smokes clove cigarettes from Indonesia.
7 The plane landed in Jakarta at 10.30 a.m.
8 They fled to a safer place.
9 She combs her daughter's hair every morning.
10 I don't understand the question.

LATIHAN 5

Here are some pictures of animals. Find **meN-** verbs to describe their sounds.

Summary

- **MeN-** verbs can be transitive or intransitive.
- **MeN-** verbs can have a noun base or a verbal base.
- In many cases, the **meN-** prefix is required for the base word to be well-formed or to make sense; in some cases, the base word cannot occur by itself.
- Some **meN-** words are adjectives rather than verbs.
- A few **meN-** verbs mean the same as their corresponding **ber-** verbs.

MeN–kan

The suffix **-kan** is often attached to **meN-** words to make them transitive. Of course, we can also have transitive verbs without the suffix **-kan,** as we saw in the previous chapters. When a prefix and a suffix are attached to the same base word, we call it a *circumfix.*

MeN–kan words are primarily verbs; a few are adjectives. They can be grouped according to the meaning that the affixation gives to the base word.

12.1 Indicating the transitive

In many cases, **meN–kan** merely indicates that the verbs are transitive. The affixation gives no other meaning except that its presence is required to make the verb well formed. For example, the verb **melakukan** (do, carry out or commit something) cannot occur without the prefix **meN-** and the suffix **-kan**. Similarly, the verb **menganjurkan** (suggest, advise) must have the affixes to make sense at all; **anjur** does not make sense by itself.

Other examples of **-kan** transitive verbs are listed below.

-KAN VERB	ENGLISH MEANING
membandingkan	to compare
membayangkan	to imagine
membicarakan	to talk about, discuss
memikirkan	to think about
mendengarkan	to listen to
menerangkan	to explain
menerjemahkan	to translate
mengabaikan	to ignore
mengadakan	to do, hold an event (for example, a party, meeting)
mengatakan	to say
mengenakan	to wear
mengerjakan	to do (for example, homework)
menjelekkan	to say bad things about someone
menyalahkan	to accuse someone of wrongdoing

Note
Sometimes we find two **meN-** verbs with the same base, but one has **-kan** while the other does not, and both are transitive. In these cases, the verbs have different meanings.

MEN- VERB	ENGLISH MEANING	**MEN–KAN** VERB	ENGLISH MEANING
meminjam	to borrow	**meminjamkan**	to lend
mendengar	to hear	**mendengarkan**	to listen to
menyewa	to rent, hire	**menyewakan**	to rent to someone

12.2 Causative

The second meaning of **meN–kan** is causative; that is, to cause something to be or become what the base word indicates. For example, the verb **membersihkan** comes from the base word **bersih** (clean). The verb can be translated literally as 'cause to become clean', but idiomatically as 'to clean'. Here are some other examples of causative **meN–kan** verbs. (Remember that all of these verbs are transitive.)

BASE WORD	ENGLISH MEANING	**MEN–KAN** VERB	ENGLISH MEANING
besar	big, large	**membesarkan**	to enlarge
dingin	cold	**mendinginkan**	to chill or cool something down
duduk	sit	**mendudukkan**	to seat someone
halus	smooth	**menghaluskan**	to make smooth
hidup	live, alive	**menghidupkan**	to turn on (example, light, television, car, stereo)
hijau	green	**menghijaukan**	to revegetate
jatuh	fall, drop	**menjatuhkan**	to drop something
kecil	small	**mengecilkan**	to turn down (for example, volume), alter something to become small (for example, pants, dress)
keluar	come/go out	**mengeluarkan**	to send or take somebody/something out (for example, of a bag or room), expel
masuk	go in, enter	**memasukkan**	to put into
mati	die, dead	**mematikan**	to turn off (for example, light, television, car, stereo)
panas	hot	**memanaskan**	to heat something up
rapi	neat, organised	**merapikan**	to tidy up (for example, bed, books)
sederhana	simple	**menyederhanakan**	to simplify
terbang	fly	**menerbangkan**	to fly something, to pilot
tidur	sleep	**menidurkan**	to put to sleep

LATIHAN 1

Complete each of the following sentences by selecting an appropriate word from the box. Each word may be used only once.

KOSAKATA

boneka	doll
desain	design
hutan	forest
mesin	engine
saku	pocket
sengaja	intentional
swasta	private, non-government

mengeluarkan	menidurkan
menghijaukan	mematikan
memasukkan	menyederhanakan
menghidupkan	menjatuhkan
merapikan	mendudukkan

1 Pak Budi ________________________ anaknya ke sekolah swasta di kota itu.
2 Pada jam 6 sore ibu ________________________ lampu di ruang tamu.
3 Tono sedang ________________________ tempat tidurnya.
4 Edi sedang ________________________ uang dari sakunya.
5 Bu Bejo akan ________________________ anaknya di kamar depan.
6 Ani ________________________ bonekanya di kursi rotan.
7 Dia dengan sengaja ________________________ botol kecap manis itu.
8 Kita harus ________________________ kembali hutan itu.
9 Mengapa dia tidak mau ________________________ mesin mobilnya?
10 Bisa anda ________________________ desain rumah itu?

12.3 Benefactive

The third meaning of **meN–kan** is *benefactive*; that is, it indicates that the action shown by the verb is done for the benefit of someone else (who is called the *beneficiary*).

The benefactive **meN–kan** often occurs in a sentence with two objects. The first object, which directly follows the verb, is called the *primary object*, while the second is called the *secondary object*. In sentences with **meN–kan**, the beneficiary appears as the primary object. The secondary object is usually referred to as the *patient*. (Remember that this is a grammatical term and does not mean the same as a patient at a hospital.) The patient is the thing that is affected by the action (e.g. being given or transferred). To help you remember which one is which, here is a simple definition of each of these terms:

- *Primary object*: Object that directly follows the verb.
- *Secondary object*: Object that follows the primary object.
- *Beneficiary*: Person who benefits from the action indicated by the verb. In **meN–kan** sentences, this is the primary object.
- *Patient*: Thing being affected by the action. In **meN–kan** sentences, this is the secondary object.

Ayah	**membuatkan**	**kami**	**teh.**
Subject	*Verb*	*Primary object*	*Secondary object*
Agent		*Beneficiary*	*Patient*
Father	made	us	tea.

Anna	**membelikan**	**ibunya**	**jaket kulit.**
Subject	*Verb*	*Primary object*	*Secondary object*
Agent		*Beneficiary*	*Patient*
Anna	bought	her mother	a leather jacket.

The sets of examples below should further clarify the benefactive use of **meN–kan**. Both sentences in each set are transitive, but only the **b** examples are benefactive.

1 a **Sita membuka pintu kamar.**
Sita opened the bedroom door.

b **Sita membukakan ibunya pintu kamar.**
(Literally: Sita opened for her mother the door.)
Sita opened the door for her mother.

2 a **John menulis surat kepada temannya.**
John wrote a letter to his friend.

b **John menuliskan saya surat.**
(Literally: John wrote for me a letter.)
John wrote a letter for me.

3 a **Rina membuat kue coklat.**
Rina made a chocolate cake.

b **Rina membuatkan ibu kue coklat.**
(Literally: Rina made for mother a chocolate cake.)
Rina made a chocolate cake for mother.

The benefactive **meN–kan** does not, however, always have two objects. When the beneficiary is known or assumed, often it is not mentioned. For example, in the following exchange, the beneficiary is B, but the word **kamu** is not mentioned. The suffix **-kan** already indicates that the action is done for someone else.

A: **Siapa yang membukakan pintu ketika kamu pulang tadi malam?**
Who opened the door (for you) when you came home last night?
B: **Bapak.**
Father.

Mentioning the beneficiary (hence mentioning **kamu** twice), as shown below, is often unnecessary.

Siapa yang membukakan <u>kamu</u> pintu ketika <u>kamu</u> pulang tadi malam?

LATIHAN 2

The following are sets of verbs with the same base word. Write a sentence in Indonesian for each verb in the set: one simple transitive and the other benefactive, as shown above. For the benefactive sentences, you can choose to mention or not mention the beneficiary.

1 a **mengambil** (get)
  b **mengambilkan** (get for someone)
2 a **menutup** (close, shut)
  b **menutupkan** (close/shut for someone)

3 a **membaca** (read)
  b **membacakan** (read for someone)
4 a **membeli** (buy)
  b **membelikan** (buy for someone)
5 a **memasak** (cook)
  b **memasakkan** (cook for someone)
6 a **membawa** (bring)
  b **membawakan** (bring for someone)
7 a **mencari** (look for)
  b **mencarikan** (look for something for someone)
8 a **mencuci** (wash)
  b **mencucikan** (wash for someone)

12.4 Optional *-kan*

In some cases, verbs with the suffix **-kan** mean the same as those without the suffix. The suffix does not lend any additional meaning to these verbs, so we can use either form. Some of these verbs are:

MEN- VERB	ENGLISH MEANING	**MEN–KAN** VERB	ENGLISH MEANING
memberi	to give	**memberikan**	to give
mendapat	to get, obtain	**mendapatkan**	to get, obtain
mengantar	to take/accompany someone to a place	**mengantarkan**	to take/accompany someone to a place

Kepala sekolah memberi(kan) penghargaan kepada murid itu.
The headmaster/headmistress gave an award to that student.

Ayahnya mendapat(kan) pekerjaan di Bandung.
Her father got a job in Bandung.

Mereka mengantar(kan) saya ke bandara.
They took me to the airport.

12.5 Undifferentiated *meN–kan* and *ber-*

In very few cases, **meN–kan** verbs are used in the same way as **ber-** verbs; that is, intransitively. One example is:

MEN–KAN VERB	ENGLISH MEANING	**BER-** VERB	ENGLISH MEANING
mengatakan	to say	**berkata**	to say

Dia mengatakan/berkata bahwa dia akan datang ke pesta saya.
He/she said that he/she would come to my party.

12.6 Contrast between *meN–kan* and *member–kan*

Some verbs suffixed by **-kan** that have the same base have different meanings, depending on whether they have the prefix **meN-** or the prefix **member-**.

MEN–KAN OR **MEMBER–KAN** VERB	ENGLISH MEANING
melakukan	to do, carry out or commit something
memberlakukan	to put something into effect (for example, sanction, regulation)
memberhentikan	to sack someone
menghentikan	to stop something

LATIHAN 3

Identify the meaning of **meN–kan** in the following sentences: simple transitive, causative or benefactive. Please note that sometimes a verb can be both simple transitive and causative, or both causative and benefactive.

1 Mereka sedang mengerjakan apa?
2 Ira akan memanaskan susu di dapur.
3 Di mana temanmu akan menghentikan mobilnya?
4 Siapa yang membelikanmu kalkulator itu?
5 Sekolah kami akan mengadakan pertandingan sepak bola.
6 Rudi sedang membacakan temannya lirik lagu itu.
7 Mengapa kamu belum membersihkan mejamu?
8 Saya tidak suka menerjemahkan kalimat dari bahasa Indonesia ke bahasa Inggris.
9 Sally tidak mau mengecilkan radionya.
10 Mereka sedang membicarakan masalah lingkungan di ruangan itu.
11 Dia mengatakan apa kepada anda?
12 Jangan menyalahkan saya kalau kamu tidak bisa ke bioskop.

LATIHAN 4

Survey five people in your class to find out who does what at home. Write their names in the left column of a table like the one shown on the next page. For each subsequent column, you must ask each person **'Siapa yang …?'** and record his or her response in the appropriate space. Present your findings to the class.

NAMA	MEMBERSIH-KAN KAMAR MANDI	MENGELUAR-KAN SAMPAH	MERAPIKAN TEMPAT TIDUR	MENGHIDUP-KAN LAMPU RUANG TAMU PADA MALAM HARI	MEMATIKAN TELEVISI PADA MALAM HARI
1					
2					
3					
4					
5					

12.7 MeN–kan adjectives

Some **meN–kan** words can be adjectives as well as verbs. These are words primarily to do with emotion or state of mind.

BASE WORD	MEN–KAN WORD	ENGLISH MEANING AS VERB	ENGLISH MEANING AS ADJECTIVE
bingung confused	**membingungkan**	to confuse someone	confusing
gembira happy, pleased	**menggembirakan**	to make someone happy or pleased	pleasing
jengkel annoyed	**menjengkelkan**	to annoy someone	annoying
kecewa disappointed	**mengecewakan**	to disappoint someone	disappointing
lega relieved	**melegakan**	to make someone relieved	cause for relief
prihatin concerned	**memprihatinkan**	to make someone concerned	cause for concern, worrisome
ragu in doubt	**meragukan**	to doubt someone or something	cause for doubt
sedih sad	**menyedihkan**	to make someone sad, sadden	saddening, pitiful
senang glad	**menyenangkan**	to make someone glad	pleasing, exciting

Note

A few **men–kan** words are either adjectives or verbs, not both.

menggiurkan	(adjective only):	enticing, tempting
memarahkan	(causative verb only):	to make someone angry, irritate

LATIHAN 5

Interview a classmate to find out about his or her likes and dislikes based on the following questions. First, translate these questions into Indonesian using **'Apa yang paling ... anda?'**. Your classmate's answers should start with **'Yang paling ... saya adalah ...'**.

1 What annoys you most?
2 What makes you happiest?
3 What confuses you most?
4 What concerns you most?
5 What saddens you most?

LATIHAN 6

KOSAKATA

batuk	cough
bercanda	joke around
bersedia	willing
kesulitan	problem
meludah	to spit
menyontek	to copy other people's work

Below are some habits or traits that we often find in people. Find a **meN–kan** adjective to describe what you think of such habits or traits in people. Rate your opinion by adding some intensifying words in front of your adjectives, such as:

tidak terlalu	not too ...
sedikit	a little ...
sangat	very ...

1 Rajin mencuci piring sesudah makan.
2 Batuk tanpa menutup mulut.
3 Meludah di mana-mana.
4 Tidak pernah mau mendengarkan orang lain.
5 Selalu tersenyum setiap kali anda bertemu dengannya.
6 Selalu bicara dengan suara keras.
7 Selalu bersedia menolong jika orang lain ada kesulitan.
8 Menyontek pekerjaan anda setiap kali ada tugas atau ujian.
9 Suka menjelekkan anda kepada teman lain.
10 Suka bercanda jika bertemu dengan anda.

LATIHAN 7

Write a simple caption in Indonesian for each of the following pictures using a **meN–kan** verb, then say whether that verb is a simple transitive, causative or benefactive.

Summary

- **MeN–kan** words are primarily transitive verbs.
- They can have causative or benefactive meaning.
- Sometimes the suffix **-kan** is optional.
- In very few cases, **meN–kan** verbs mean the same as their corresponding **ber-** verbs.
- Verbs affixed with **meN–kan** have different meanings than those affixed with **member–kan.**
- Some **meN–kan** words are adjectives as well as verbs. A few **meN–kan** words are either adjectives or verbs, not both.

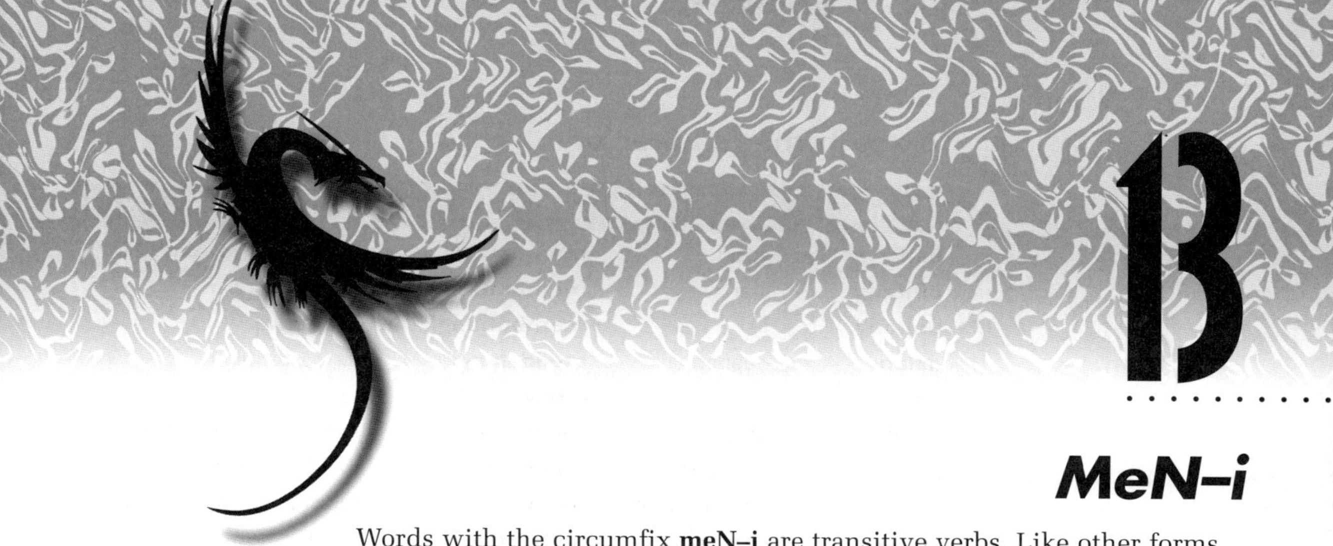

13

MeN–i

Words with the circumfix **meN–i** are transitive verbs. Like other forms of affixation, **meN–i** gives different meanings when attached to the base word. In this chapter we look at some of these meanings.

Unlike **meN–kan** words, which include transitive verbs and adjectives, **meN–i** words are only transitive verbs. There are no **meN–i** adjectives.

The main point to remember about **meN–i** verbs is that the object that directly follows the verb is conceptualised as a static location; that is, the object does not change location. Some examples later in this chapter will clarify this further.

13.1 Various meanings of *meN–i* verbs

To apply or take off

BASE WORD	ENGLISH MEANING	**MEN–I** VERB	ENGLISH MEANING
air	water	**mengairi**	to water (rice field, not garden)
gambar	picture	**menggambari**	to draw a picture on something
gula	sugar	**menggulai**	to sweeten
kulit	skin	**menguliti**	to skin something
minyak	oil	**meminyaki**	to oil
obat	medication	**mengobati**	to treat with medication
sisik	scale	**menyisiki**	to scale (for example, fish)
tandatangan	signature	**menandatangani**	to sign
warna	colour	**mewarnai**	to colour in

To act in the manner of

BASE WORD	ENGLISH MEANING	**MEN–I** VERB	ENGLISH MEANING
baik	good	**membaiki**	to be good to someone
bintang	star	**membintangi**	to star in a film
bohong	lie	**membohongi**	to deceive
dalang	puppeteer	**mendalangi**	to mastermind
guru	teacher	**menggurui**	to patronise
jahat	bad, evil	**menjahati**	to treat someone badly
juara	champion	**menjuarai**	to win (games)
kasih	love, affection	**mengasihi**	to love, have affection for
ketua	chairperson	**mengetuai**	to chair, head
musuh	enemy	**memusuhi**	to treat as enemy
raja	king	**merajai**	to rule over
sponsor	sponsor	**mensponsori**	to sponsor
sutradara	film director	**menyutradarai**	to direct (films)
wakil	representative	**mewakili**	to represent

To cause something to become what is indicated by the base word

BASE WORD	ENGLISH MEANING	**MEN–I** VERB	ENGLISH MEANING
basah	wet	**membasahi**	to wet
kotor	dirty	**mengotori**	to dirty
kurang	less	**mengurangi**	to reduce
luka	wound	**melukai**	to hurt (physical or emotional)

Repeated action

Some **meN–i** verbs indicate that the action is done repeatedly to one or more objects.

BASE WORD	ENGLISH MEANING	**MEN–I** VERB	ENGLISH MEANING
ambil	get, take	**mengambili**	to get or take things
bakar	burn	**membakari**	to burn land or things
cium	kiss	**menciumi**	to kiss repeatedly
garuk	scratch	**menggaruki**	to scratch repeatedly
gigit	bite	**menggigiti**	to bite repeatedly
pukul	hit	**memukuli**	to hit repeatedly
tebang	fell (trees)	**menebangi**	to fell many trees

13.2 Contrast between *meN–i* and *meN–kan* verbs

Some **meN–i** and **meN–kan** verbs with the same base word have different meanings depending on how the object (the primary object, if there are two objects in the sentence) is perceived or conceptualised. As mentioned at the beginning of this chapter, the object in sentences with **meN–i** verbs is conceptualised as a static location; it does not change location. In contrast, the object in sentences with **meN–kan** verbs changes location; it moves from one place to another.

Notice below that in **1a** the object (**saya**) is stationary, while in **1b** the object (**radio itu**) changes location from where Bu Ratih had it before to a location closer to the table.

1	a	**Bu Ratih**	**mendekati**	**saya**	**siang tadi.**
		Subject	*Verb*	*Object*	*Adverb of time*
		Bu Ratih	approached	me	this afternoon.
	b	**Bu Ratih**	**mendekatkan**	**radio itu**	**ke meja saya.**
		Subject	*Verb*	*Object*	*Prepositional phrase*
		Bu Ratih	brought	the radio	closer to my table.
2	a	**Ibu**	**mengantari**	**Bu Marni**	**kue.**
		Subject	*Verb*	*Beneficiary*	*Patient*
		Mother	brought	Bu Marni	a cake.
		→ Bu Marni stays where she is.			
	b	**Ibu**	**mengantarkan**	**kue**	**untuk Bu Marni.**
		Subject	*Verb*	*Patient*	*Prepositional phrase*
		Mother	brought	a cake	for Bu Marni.
		→ The cake changes location from Mother's hands to Bu Marni's.			
3	a	**Ahmad**	**menyirami**	**kebunnya**	**setiap sore.**
		Subject	*Verb*	*Object*	*Adverb of frequency*
		Ahmad	waters	his garden	every afternoon.
		→ The garden stays where it is.			
	b	**Ahmad**	**menyiramkan**	**seember air**	**ke pohon itu.**
		Subject	*Verb*	*Object*	*Prepositional phrase*
		Ahmad	poured	a bucket of water	on the tree.
		→ The water changes location from the bucket in Ahmad's hands to the tree.			

LATIHAN 1

The following pairs of sentences contain **meN–i** and **meN–kan** verbs. Draw a simple picture to illustrate each sentence, showing whether the object remains stationary or changes location.

1 **a** Saya akan pergi sebentar; jangan menduduki kursi saya ya.
  b Adik mendudukkan bonekanya di tempat tidur.
2 **a** Mereka mengantari saya bunga kemarin.
  b Pak Harsoyo mengantarkan anaknya ke dokter gigi.
3 **a** Dia menjauhi anjing yang galak itu.
  b Bapak menjauhkan pisau tajam itu dari jangkauan anaknya.
4 **a** Mereka berenang menyeberangi sungai itu.
  b Petugas menyeberangkan anak-anak sekolah setiap pagi.
5 **a** Bu Rani menanami kebunnya dengan jagung.
  b Bu Rani menanamkan biji jagung di kebunnya.
6 **a** Kakak menghadiahi ibu topi wol untuk ulang tahunnya.
  b Pak Diman menghadiahkan sepeda kepada anaknya.
7 **a** Dokter mengobati pasien kanker itu.
  b Mereka pergi mengobatkan anaknya ke dokter.
8 **a** Mereka menaburi makam neneknya dengan bunga.
  b Mereka menaburkan bunga di makam neneknya.

KOSAKATA (KATA DASAR = BASE WORD)

antar	to take something/someone somewhere
duduk	to sit
hadiah	gift
jauh	far
makam	grave
obat	medication
seberang	across
tabur	to sprinkle
tanam	to sow

KOSAKATA LAIN (OTHER VOCABULARY)

boneka	doll
galak	ferocious
jangkauan	to reach
pisau	knife
sungai	river
tajam	sharp
ulang tahun	birthday
wol	wool

13.3 Undifferentiated *meN–i* and *meN–kan*

Sometimes Indonesian speakers do not differentiate between **meN–i** and **meN–kan**, which can be confusing for some learners. Fortunately, there are not too many cases where this occurs. Here are some examples.

MEN–I VERB	ENGLISH MEANING	MEN–KAN VERB	ENGLISH MEANING
memanasi	to heat (for example, food, milk)	**memanaskan**	to heat (for example, food, milk)
memberati	to trouble or cause anxiety	**memberatkan**	to trouble or cause anxiety
memikiri	to think about	**memikirkan**	to think about
menamai	to name	**menamakan**	to name
mengingini	to want, desire	**menginginkan**	to want, desire
menyakiti	to hurt (feelings)	**menyakitkan**	to hurt (feelings)

LATIHAN 2

Translate the following sentences with **meN–i** and **meN–kan** into English.

1 Tadi malam polisi mendatangi rumah kami.
2 Produser film itu mendatangkan aktor dari luar negeri.
3 Ibu saya sedih memikirkan adik saya yang tidak mau sekolah.
4 Dillah memasukkan uang itu ke dompetnya.
5 Para demonstran melemparkan batu ke kantor itu dengan marah.
6 Pencuri mulai mengambili barang-barang di rumah itu.
7 Siapa yang akan mengantarkan kamu ke sekolah besok?
8 Jane menangisi anjingnya yang mati.
9 Siapa yang meniduri tempat tidur itu tadi malam?
10 Bapak menaiki tangga itu pelan-pelan.

13.4 Other *meN–i* and *meN–kan* contrasts

Some other **meN–i** and **meN–kan** words share the same base word but no obvious contrast in meaning, unlike those we saw in section 13.2. The best way to remember them might just be to learn them by heart.

MEN–I OR MEN–KAN VERB	ENGLISH MEANING
memperingati	to commemorate
memperingatkan	to warn, reprimand
mendahului	to overtake, to beat someone in something
mendahulukan	to put something or someone first
menyelamati	to congratulate
menyelamatkan	to save someone or something

13.5 *MeN–i* and corresponding intransitive verbs

As discussed in Chapter 9, in some cases an intransitive verb can be transformed into a transitive verb by using **meN-** verbs suffixed either by **-i** or **-kan**. The meaning may be similar or it may change. Here are some examples with **meN–i**.

INTRANSITIVE VERB + PREPOSITION	ENGLISH MEANING	MEN–KAN TRANSITIVE VERB	ENGLISH MEANING
berdiam di	to live in	**mendiami**	to occupy, inhabit
bertemu dengan	to meet with	**menemui**	to go and see someone
duduk di	to sit on	**menduduki**	to occupy a position or territory
hadir di	to be present at, attend	**menghadiri**	to attend
marah kepada	to be angry with	**memarahi**	to be angry with, scold
masuk ke	to go into, enter	**memasuki**	to go into, enter
menikah dengan	to get married to	**menikahi**	to wed
percaya kepada	to believe in	**mempercayai**	to believe in, trust
sadar akan	to be aware of, conscious of	**menyadari**	to realise
suka akan/dengan	to like, be fond of	**menyukai**	to like, favour
tahu tentang	to know about	**mengetahui**	to know something

LATIHAN 3

Translate the following sentences into Indonesian using either intransitive or transitive verbs with **meN–i**.

1 I don't believe in ghosts.
2 I realised that I was wrong.
3 They trusted me to buy the computer.
4 Ali went to see the headmistress.
5 He married a girl from Surabaya.
6 The Japanese occupied Indonesia from 1942 to 1945.
7 They know my weakness.
8 Twelve million people inhabit that territory.
9 Don't be angry with me.
10 They attended the protest last week.

KOSAKATA	
hantu	ghost
kelemahan	weakness
kepala sekolah	head-mistress
protes	protest

LATIHAN 4

Look at the following pictures, then write a simple caption for each one in Indonesian using either **meN–i** or **meN–kan** verbs.

Summary

- Words with **meN–i** are transitive verbs.
- The object of **meN–i** verbs is conceptualised as a static location.
- The **meN–i** affixation gives different meanings to the base word.
- Contrast between **MeN–i** and **meN–kan** verbs:
  —Some are contrasted in meaning: the object in **meN–i** does not change location, while in **meN–kan** it does.
  —Some **meN–i** and **meN–kan** verbs are not differentiated in meaning, while some others are.
  —Some **meN–i** verbs have corresponding intransitive verbs. Some of them have similar meanings, while others are quite different.

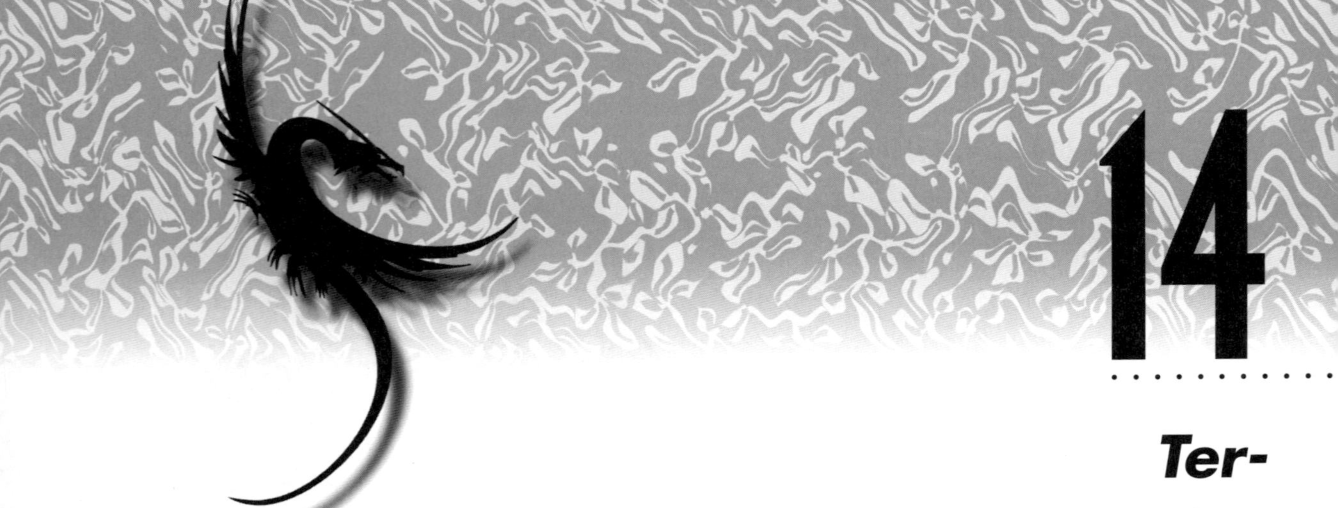

14 Ter-

Words prefixed by **ter-** fall into two main categories: adjectives and verbs. The adjectives are easier to remember because they have only one general meaning, while the verbs have several meanings.

14.1 Adjective *ter-*

When **ter-** is affixed to adjectives, it indicates superlative, which in English is shown by the word 'most' (for example, 'most important', 'most expensive') or the ending '-est' (for example, 'smartest', 'easiest', 'coldest'). **Ter-** in this use can be substituted by the word **paling**, which means the same thing, as shown below.

TER- SUPERLATIVE	ENGLISH MEANING	**PALING** SUPERLATIVE	ENGLISH MEANING
terbaik	best	**paling baik**	best
terbaru	newest	**paling baru**	newest
tercanggih	most sophisticated/ modern (for example, of technology)	**paling canggih**	most sophisticated/ modern (for example, of technology)
tercantik	most beautiful	**paling cantik**	most beautiful
tercepat	fastest, quickest	**paling cepat**	fastest, quickest
terkaya	richest	**paling kaya**	richest
termahal	most expensive	**paling mahal**	most expensive
termodern	most modern	**paling modern**	most modern
termudah	easiest	**paling mudah**	easiest
termurah	cheapest	**paling murah**	cheapest
terpandai	smartest, cleverest	**paling pandai**	smartest, cleverest
tertinggi	tallest, highest	**paling tinggi**	tallest, highest

LATIHAN 1

Answer the following questions in Indonesian.

1 Siapa orang yang terkaya di dunia?

2 Binatang apa yang tercepat larinya?
3 Gunung apa yang tertinggi di dunia?
4 Toko apa yang termurah di koto anda?
5 Apa judul film yang terbaru bulan ini?

14.2 *Ter-* verbs

Verbs prefixed by **ter-** are either *stative verbs*, indicating no action, or *action verbs* (intransitive or transitive), indicating action. Action verbs describe either accidental action or abilitative action.

Stative verbs

'Stative' means that the verbs do not suggest any action; they mainly indicate a state of affairs.

TER- VERB	ENGLISH MEANING
terbagi	divided
terbalik	upside down, inside out, back to front
terbuka	opened
tercatat	noted, listed
terdaftar	registered, enrolled
terdapat	found
tergantung	hung (for example, painting, lamp)
terkenal	well-known
terletak	located
terpenuhi	fulfilled
terpuruk	hidden, buried, in worst state
terputus	broken
tersirat	implied
tertata	organised, neatly put
tertempel	stuck (for example, poster on wall, sticker on book)
tertera	listed
tertulis	written
tertutup	shut, closed

LATIHAN 2

Complete the following sentences with words from the above list.

1 Jakarta ________________________ di pulau Jawa.
2 Namanya sudah ________________________ di daftar kelas.
3 Poster besar itu ________________________ di dinding kamar saya.
4 Perabot rumahnya semua ________________________ rapi.
5 Biarkan jendela itu ________________________ karena hawa di ruangan ini panas sekali.
6 Aduh, kaki saya sakit sekali karena ________________________

KOSAKATA

biarkan	to let
daftar	list
dinding	wall
hawa	air, temperature
perabot	furniture
rapi	neat

Accidental action: intransitive

Ter- verbs can be either intransitive or transitive. The verbs in the following table are intransitive. This means that they take a subject but no object. When used as intransitive, **ter-** suggests the following meanings.

- The subject experiences some forced or involuntary motion.
- The subject displays spontaneous expressions.

FORCED OR INVOLUNTARY MOTION

TER- VERB	ENGLISH MEANING
terbentur	hit, knocked (usually the head)
terduduk	to fall into sitting position
tergelincir	to skid, slip
terguncang	shaken
terjatuh	to fall
terjerembab	to fall flat on one's face
terjerumus	to fall into a trap or hole
terlempar	flung
terpelanting	darted off, flipped over
terperosok	to sink into, slip into
tersandung	to stumble, trip over
tersasar	lost (lose one's way)

SPONTANEOUS EXPRESSIONS

TER- VERB	ENGLISH MEANING
terdiam	to fall silent
ternganga	having one's mouth agape
terpaku	transfixed (literally 'nailed')
tersenyum	to smile
tertawa	to laugh
tertegun	startled, stunned

Lina	**terjatuh**	**dari tangga.**
Subject	*Verb*	*Prepositional phrase*
Lina	fell	off the stairs.

Anak itu	**tersenyum**	**manis.**
Subject	*Verb*	*Adverb*
The child	smiled	sweetly.

LATIHAN 3

Work in pairs, taking turns to act out the following words while your partner tries to guess what the word is in Indonesian.

1 Terduduk
2 Tertawa
3 Tersandung
4 Terbentur
5 Ternganga
6 Tersenyum
7 Tergelincir
8 Terdiam

Accidental action: transitive

The following **ter-** verbs are used in the sentence preceded by an object, much like the object-focus (passive)—see Chapter 19. **Ter-** in this use suggests the following meanings.

- The object experiences something that it cannot control.
- The object experiences something done by mistake.

UNCONTROLLABLE EVENT

TER- VERB	ENGLISH MEANING
terbangun	woken
tergeser	pushed aside
terinjak	stepped on
terkecoh	defrauded, deceived
terpergok	caught red-handed
terpukul	hit (by someone)
tertabrak	hit by something (for example, car)
tertangkap	caught, captured
tertipu	cheated, deceived

SOMETHING DONE BY MISTAKE

TER- VERB	ENGLISH MEANING
terbawa	taken by mistake
termakan	eaten by mistake

Saya	**terbangun**	**oleh**	**suara keras**	**di luar.**
Object	*Verb*	*by*	*Subject*	*Prepositional phrase*
I	was woken up	by	a loud noise	outside.
Mobilnya	**tertabrak**	**oleh**	**truk**	**di jalan tol.**
Object	*Verb*	*by*	*Subject*	*Prepositional phrase*
Her car	was hit	by	a truck	on the tollway.

You can also leave out the 'by phrase' if you wish. In conversation, people often do this. When the addressee wants to know further, he or she can ask for more specific information. For instance, we can just say:

Mobilnya tertabrak.
Her car was hit.

If our addressee wants to know who or what hit the car, he or she can ask:

Oleh siapa?
By whom?

or:

Siapa yang menabrak?
Who hit it?

Abilitative

'Abilitative' means 'able to be (can be) what the base word indicates'. The verbs below can also be used as transitive in a manner similar to the object-focus (passive) discussed above.

TER- VERB	ENGLISH MEANING
terbeli	can be afforded
tercium	can be smelt
terdengar	audible
teringat	comes to mind (recalled)
terjangkau	can be reached
terlihat	visible
terpikir	comes to mind (thought about)

Baju mahal itu	**tak**	**terbeli**	**oleh**	**saya.**
Object	*Negative*	*Verb*	*by*	*Subject*
I	cannot	afford	that	expensive shirt.

(Literally: That expensive shirt cannot be bought by me.)

As in the previous transitive example, you can also omit the 'by' phrase.

Suaranya	**tidak**	**terdengar.**
Object	*Negative*	*Verb*
His voice	cannot	be heard (inaudible).

LATIHAN 4

Choose the correct answer for each of the following sentences.

1 Tidak ... oleh saya untuk membawa payung.
  a terbawa
  b terpikir
  c terlihat

KOSAKATA

berdarah dingin cold-blooded
kas cash register
payung umbrella
pembunuh murderer
penuh sesak absolutely full, 'chock-a-block'

2 Penjaga toko itu ... mencuri uang dari kas.
 a teringat
 b terpergok
 c terkecoh
3 Baru ... olehnya bahwa hari ini adalah hari ulang tahun ibunya.
 a tertangkap
 b terpikir
 c teringat
4 Karena bis penuh sesak, kaki saya ... oleh orang.
 a telihat
 b tergeser
 c terinjak
5 Pembunuh berdarah dingin itu sampai sekarang belum ...
 a tertabrak
 b tertangkap
 c tertipu

14.3 Other uses

There are **ter-** words that do not fit into the categories above.

TER- WORD	ENGLISH MEANING
terdiri (dari, atas)	to consist (of)
terhadap	towards (a person)
terlalu	too (followed by an adjective), similar to **ke–an** with the 'excessiveness' meaning
terlambat	late
termasuk	include
terpaksa	to be forced to
terserah	as you will, up to you

14.4 *Ter-* and *ke-* or *ke–an*

Ter- is often replaced by either **ke-** or **ke–an**, with no difference in meaning. The only difference is that **ter-** sounds more formal, whereas **ke-** and **ke–an** are less formal and are more often used in spoken Indonesian.

Ter- is replaceable by **ke-** or **ke–an** particularly in transitive verbs.

Ter- = *ke-*

TER- VERB	ENGLISH MEANING	**KE-** VERB	ENGLISH MEANING
terbangun	to be woken by something	**kebangun**	to be woken by something
terbeli	can be bought, can be afforded	**kebeli**	can be bought, can be afforded
tercium	can be smelt	**kecium**	can be smelt
tergeser	to be shifted or to be pushed aside	**kegeser**	to be shifted or to be pushed aside
terinjak	to be accidentally stepped on	**keinjak**	to be accidentally stepped on
terjangkau	can be reached, affordable	**kejangkau**	can be reached, affordable
terpergok	caught red-handed	**kepergok**	caught red-handed
terpikir	to come to mind	**kepikir**	to come to mind
terpukul	to be accidentally hit by someone or to be psychologically affected by some event	**kepukul**	to be accidentally hit by someone or to be psychologically affected by some event
tersasar	to lose one's way	**kesasar**	to lose one's way
tertabrak	to be accidentally hit by a vehicle	**ketabrak**	to be accidentally hit by a vehicle
tertangkap	to be caught, to be captured	**ketangkap**	to be caught, to be captured
tertawa	to laugh	**ketawa**	to laugh
tertipu	to be cheated, to be conned	**ketipu**	to be cheated, to be conned

Ter- = *ke–an*

TER- VERB	ENGLISH MEANING	**KE–AN** VERB	ENGLISH MEANING
terdengar	audible	**kedengaran**	audible
terlihat	visible	**kelihatan**	visible

Did you know?
To say that someone is a victim of gossip (believing gossip), you can use the expression **termakan gosip**, literally meaning 'to be eaten by gossip'.

14.5 Reduplicated *ter-*

Ter- verbs in this group usually describe manner.

TER- VERB	ENGLISH MEANING
terbahak-bahak	roaring (with laughter)
tergesa-gesa	in a hurry (walking or running)
terkantuk-kantuk	to nod off (in sleepiness)
tersipu-sipu	shyly (of facial expression)

Dia terbahak-bahak ketika mendengar cerita saya.
He/she roared with laughter when hearing my story.

Sometimes Indonesian speakers add another verb in front of these **ter-** verbs. However, the English translation remains the same.

Dia tertawa terbahak-bahak ketika mendengar cerita saya.
He/she roared with laughter when hearing my story.

LATIHAN 5

Create a short story in Indonesian using all of the **ter-** words in each of the following groups.

1. Terbahak-bahak
   Terbentur
   Tergelincir
   Tergesa-gesa
   Tersandung
   Tertutup
2. Terbangun
   Terjerembab
   Terpergok
   Tersenyum
   Tersipu-sipu
   Tertidur

Summary

Uses of **ter-**

- Adjective: superlative (meaning 'most')
- Verb:
  —Stative
  —Accidental action (intransitive): forced/involuntary motion, spontaneous expressions
  —Accidental action (transitive): uncontrollable event, something done by mistake
  —Abilitative (transitive)
- Other uses
  —Ter- with a similar meaning to **ke-** or **ke–an**
  —Reduplicated **ter-** to describe manner

15

Ke–an

In grammatical terms, **ke–an** is called a *circumfix*; that is, a combination of a prefix (**ke-**) and a suffix (**-an**) to form a word. This chapter looks at the various uses of **ke–an**.

15.1 *Ke–an* verbs

Many **ke–an** verbs indicate that the subject experiences or suffers from something over which the subject has no control—similar to one of the meanings of **ter-** in Chapter 14. This meaning can be specified further, as follows.

Suffer from climatic or bodily conditions

BASE WORD	ENGLISH MEANING	**KE–AN** VERB	ENGLISH MEANING
banjir	flood	**kebanjiran**	to be caught in flood
candu	drugs	**kecanduan**	to be addicted to something
dingin	cold	**kedinginan**	to suffer from cold
haus	thirsty	**kehausan**	to be thirsty, parched
hujan	rain	**kehujanan**	to be caught in the rain
kering	dry	**kekeringan**	to suffer from drought
lapar	hungry	**kelaparan**	to be starved
panas	hot	**kepanasan**	to suffer from heat
semut	ant	**kesemutan**	to get pins and needles (literally 'to be struck or overcome by ants')

LATIHAN 1

Complete each of the following sentences using one of the **ke–an** words from the above list.

1 Beberapa negara di Afrika sangat membutuhkan hujan. Sudah beberapa bulan ini mereka menderita ______________________.

2 Aduh, saya tidak bisa berdiri karena kaki saya ______________________.

3 Kasihan Ani, dia menggigil ('shivering') ________________.
4 Ibu menghidupkan AC di ruang tamu karena merasa ________________.
5 Karena hujan yang tidak berhenti selama berhari-hari, rumah saya ________________.

Lack of control over emotions

BASE WORD	ENGLISH MEANING	KE–AN VERB	ENGLISH MEANING
senang	glad	**kesenangan**	to be overcome by glee, overjoyed
susah	sad	**kesusahan**	to be overcome by hardship
takut	afraid	**ketakutan**	to be overcome by fear, scared

Lack of control over a situation or event

BASE WORD	ENGLISH MEANING	KE–AN VERB	ENGLISH MEANING
bagi	to distribute	**kebagian**	to be given a share of something
betul	correct	**kebetulan**	by chance, it so happens
copet	pickpocket	**kecopetan**	to have one's pocket picked
curi	to steal	**kecurian**	to have something stolen
habis	finished	**kehabisan**	to run out of something
hilang	to disappear	**kehilangan**	to lose something
jatuh	fall	**kejatuhan**	to be hit by an object falling from above
maling	intruder	**kemalingan**	to have the house broken into
tahu	to know	**ketahuan**	to be caught red-handed
tidur	sleep	**ketiduran**	to fall asleep

LATIHAN 2

Translate the following sentences into English.

1 Kebetulan saya bertemu dengannya di toko sepatu itu.
2 Kasihan Joni, rumahnya kemalingan tadi malam.
3 Mereka berhasil membawa lari uang Rp5 juta tanpa ketahuan pemilik rumah.
4 Kami kehabisan beras, jadi malam ini harus berbelanja.
5 Pencuri itu lari ketakutan setelah melihat polisi datang.

KOSAKATA

berhasil	to succeed in
pemilik	owner
tanpa	without

In some cases, **ke–an** words simply indicate that something can be what the base word indicates.

BASE WORD	ENGLISH MEANING	KE–AN WORD	ENGLISH MEANING
lihat	to see	**kelihatan**	visible

In this case, the meaning of **ke–an** is similar to the abilitative meaning of the prefix **ter-** (see Chapter 14). Interestingly, **kelihatan** also extends to 'look, it seems, it looks like' when we add **-nya** at the end.

> **Kelihatannya dia sakit.**
> She looks sick.
>
> **Hari ini mendung. Kelihatannya akan hujan.**
> Today is cloudy. It looks like it's going to rain.
>
> **Kelihatannya ekonomi Indonesia akan membaik.**
> It looks like the Indonesian economy will improve.

15.2 *Ke–an* adjectives

Ke—an words in this group generally indicate 'excessiveness' and translate into English as 'too + adjective' (for example, too small, too large). They also mean the same as '**terlalu** (too) + adjective' in Indonesian (for example, **terlalu kecil**, **terlalu besar**). The difference between using **ke—an** and **terlalu** is that **ke–an** can sometimes sound more informal.

BASE WORD	ENGLISH MEANING	KE–AN ADJECTIVE	ENGLISH MEANING
besar	large	**kebesaran**	too large, too big
capai	tired	**kecapaian**	too tired, exhausted
gemuk	fat	**kegemukan**	too fat
kecil	small	**kekecilan**	too small
kenyang	full	**kekenyangan**	too full (overeating)
kurus	thin	**kekurusan**	too thin (of body)
mahal	expensive	**kemahalan**	too expensive
murah	cheap	**kemurahan**	too cheap
panjang	long	**kepanjangan**	too long
pendek	short	**kependekan**	too short
rendah	low	**kerendahan**	too low
tebal	thick	**ketebalan**	too thick
tinggi	high	**ketinggian**	too high
tipis	thin	**ketipisan**	too thin (not for body)

When **ke—an** is applied to base words indicating a particular part of the day, such as morning, afternoon or night, it means 'something happens at an inappropriate time'. For example, coming home too late at night or ringing someone too early in the morning.

BASE WORD	ENGLISH MEANING	**KE–AN** ADJECTIVE	ENGLISH MEANING
malam	night	**kemalaman**	too late (at night)
pagi	morning	**kepagian**	too early (in the morning)
siang	afternoon	**kesiangan**	too late (in the day), oversleep (get up too late)
sore	evening	**kesorean**	too late (in the afternoon)

Handy expression

A useful word to know with the 'excessiveness' meaning is **keterlaluan**, which means 'too much, too far, (of behaviour)'. It comes from **terlalu** ('too').

> **Dia memang keterlaluan. Sudah berkali-kali diperingatkan jangan terlambat, tapi masih juga begitu.**
> He/she has indeed gone too far. I've warned him/her repeatedly not to be late, but he/she still does it.

LATIHAN 3

Match these sentences with the following pictures.

1 Rok itu kebesaran.
2 Rok itu kemahalan; uang saya tidak cukup.
3 Anjing itu ketakutan.
4 Joni ketiduran di kelas.

Lihat betapa tajamnya pe-
dang... ini...

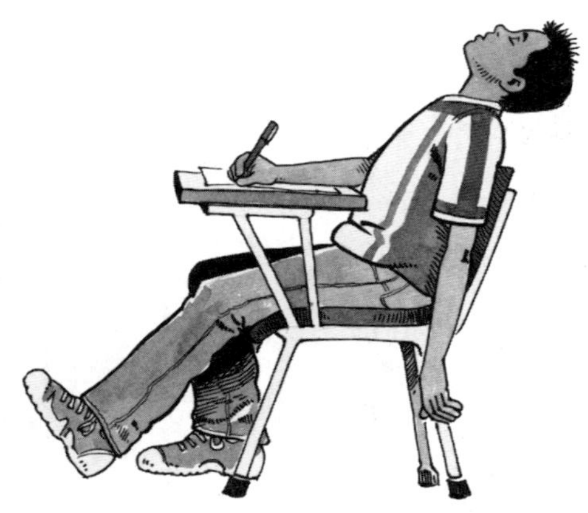

15.3 *Ke–an* abstract nouns

Ke—an also forms abstract nouns. By 'abstract' we mean things that we cannot touch, see or feel.

BASE WORD	ENGLISH MEANING	KE–AN NOUN	ENGLISH MEANING
bahagia	happy	**kebahagiaan**	happiness
bersih	clean	**kebersihan**	cleanliness
cantik	beautiful	**kecantikan**	beauty
cepat	fast	**kecepatan**	speed, velocity
duduk	to sit	**kedudukan**	position, rank
gembira	joyful	**kegembiraan**	joyfulness, excitement
giat	active	**kegiatan**	activity
hidup	live	**kehidupan**	life
kacau	mixed up	**kekacauan**	havoc
kuat	strong	**kekuatan**	strength, power
lisan	oral	**kelisanan**	orality, oracy
maju	to go forward	**kemajuan**	progress, advancement
mati	to die	**kematian**	death
puas	satisfied	**kepuasan**	satisfaction
satu	one	**kesatuan**	unity
sehat	healthy	**kesehatan**	health

We can also attach **ke—an** to words that already have a prefix, such as **ber-**. For example, the word **berada** (to be at a place) comes from the base word **ada** (there is/are, exist)and the prefix **ber-**. When we add **ke—an**, we get **keberadaan**, which means 'existence'.

Below are more examples.

BASE WORD	ENGLISH MEANING	KE–AN NOUN	ENGLISH MEANING
beraksara	literate	**keberaksaraan**	literacy
bersama	together	**kebersamaan**	togetherness

Did you know?
We can also form longer **ke—an** abstract nouns by adding the negative word **tidak** before the base word.

TIDAK + BASE WORD	ENGLISH MEANING	KE–AN NOUN	ENGLISH MEANING
Tidak adil	not fair	**ketidakadilan**	injustice
Tidak mengerti	not understand	**ketidakmengertian**	incomprehension
Tidak pasti	not certain	**ketidakpastian**	uncertainty
Tidak tahu	not know	**ketidaktahuan**	ignorance

15.4 *Ke–an* words with dual meanings

Some **ke—an** words have two meanings. Depending on how we use them, they may indicate one thing or the other.

KE–AN WORD	ADJECTIVE	ABSTRACT NOUN
kelaparan	struck by hunger	hunger
kepanjangan	too long	unabbreviated form (for example, of a name)
kependekan	too short	abbreviated form
kerendahan	too low	lowness
ketinggian	too high	height

KE–AN WORD	QUANTITY WORD	QUANTITY WORD
kebanyakan	too much, too many	most

LATIHAN 4

Match each Indonesian sentence in the left column with its English equivalent in the right column.

1 Kasihan adikmu, dia kecapaian.
2 Kegembiraannya meluap-luap.
3 Jangan makan terlalu banyak, nanti kamu kekenyangan.
4 Mobil itu melaju dengan kecepatan 90 km per jam menuju Canberra.
5 Kedudukan ibu saya di perusahaan itu adalah sebagai direktur.
6 Kemarin saya kecopetan ketika di bis.
7 Wah, saya malu sekali tadi pagi di kelas karena saya ketiduran ketika guru saya berbicara.
8 Teman saya kelihatan sedih sekali hari ini.
9 Barang siapa ketahuan menyontek dalam ujian ini akan mendapat nol.
10 Maaf Bu, saya sedang kesulitan uang, jadi belum bisa membayar sewa rumah.

a Don't overeat, or you will be bloated.
b I feel sorry for your younger sibling; he/she is exhausted.
c My mother's position in the company is director.
d Literally: His joy is overflowing. (He is over the moon.)
e The car moves at a speed of 90 kilometres per hour in the direction of Canberra.
f My friend is looking very sad today.
g I'm sorry, ma'am, I'm having a financial hardship, so I haven't been able to pay my (house) rent.
h Whoever is found cheating in this exam will get zero.
i I was so embarrassed this morning in class because I fell asleep while my teacher was talking.
j Yesterday I had my pocket picked when I was on the bus.

Summary

Uses of **ke–an**:

- **Ke–an** verbs: Generally indicating lack of control; for example, over climatic or bodily condition, emotion or over an event or situation. When attached to base words indicating parts of the day, **ke–an** indicates that something happens at an inappropriate time.
- **Ke–an** adjectives: generally indicating excessiveness (in English: 'too …')
- **Ke–an** abstract nouns
- Some **ke–an** words have dual meanings.

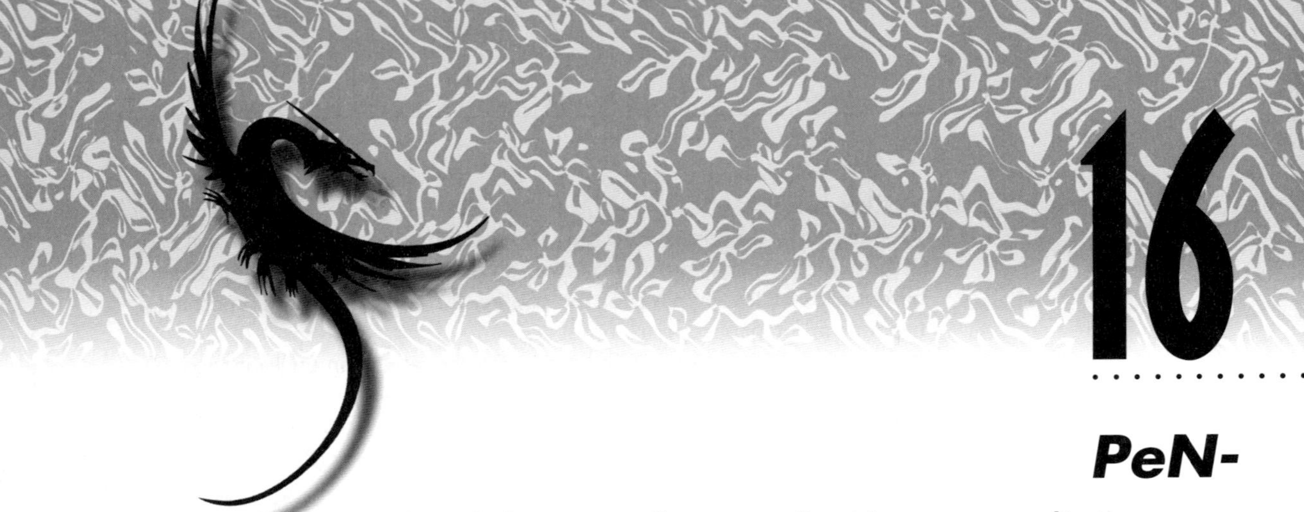

16 PeN-

Words with the **peN-** prefix are usually either nouns or adjectives.

The capital letter **N** in **peN-** indicates the same sound changes that occur in **meN-**verbs. Indeed, many **peN-** words have corresponding **meN-** verbs.

The **(N)** is written in parentheses because in some cases there are no sound changes; for example, in words that may have corresponding **ber-** verbs.

16.1 PeN- nouns

PeN- nouns are derived from various base words that are either verbs, nouns or adjectives.

A person who does, or is associated with, what the base word indicates

BASE WORD	ENGLISH MEANING	PEN- NOUN	ENGLISH MEANING
baca	to read	**pembaca**	reader
bantu	to help	**pembantu**	helper, servant
beli	to buy	**pembeli**	buyer
besar	big	**pembesar**	important government official
bohong	to lie	**pembohong**	liar
bual	to boast, brag	**pembual**	bragger
candu	illegal drugs	**pecandu**	drug addict
cinta	love	**pencinta**	lover of something
curi	to steal	**pencuri**	thief
datang	to come	**pendatang**	migrant
dengar	to hear, listen	**pendengar**	listener
jaga	to take care	**penjaga**	caretaker, keeper
jahat	evil, wicked	**penjahat**	criminal
jajah	to colonise	**penjajah**	coloniser
jual	to sell	**penjual**	seller

BASE WORD	ENGLISH MEANING	PEN- NOUN	ENGLISH MEANING
mabuk	drunk	**pemabuk**	drunkard, alcoholic
makan	to eat	**pemakan**	eater
minum	to drink	**peminum**	drinker (alcoholic)
muda	young	**pemuda**	young man, youth
pungut	to pick up, collect	**pemungut**	collector
syair	poem	**penyair**	poet
tulis	to write	**penulis**	writer

Some words do not undergo sound changes. Often, these are words that have corresponding **ber-** verbs.

BASE WORD	ENGLISH MEANING	PEN- NOUN	ENGLISH MEANING
dagang	to trade	**pedagang**	trader
gulat	to wrestle	**pegulat**	wrestler
jalan	to walk	**pejalan (kaki)**	pedestrian
kerja	to work	**pekerja**	worker
renang	to swim	**perenang**	swimmer
tenis	to play tennis	**petenis**	tennis player
tinju	to box	**petinju**	boxer

In some cases, the meaning of the **peN-** word is a metaphorical one. For example, the word **penduduk** does not mean 'person who sits', but rather 'person who occupies'; that is, 'inhabitant'.

BASE WORD	ENGLISH MEANING	PEN- NOUN	ENGLISH MEANING
duduk	to sit	**penduduk**	inhabitant, population

LATIHAN 1

Here are some pictures of people associated with certain activities or professions. Match each of the following **peN-** words with the corresponding picture.

1 Pelari
2 Pelukis
3 Pemain sepak bola
4 Pemancing ikan
5 Pendayung

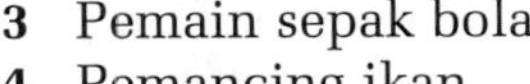

Be careful!

Although **peN-** and **per-** often mean 'the person who does something associated with the base word', they cannot be applied to all cases. For instance, the Indonesian word for 'chef' is **tukang masak**, not **pemasak**. The word **tukang** means 'person skilled in a certain area, or labourer'. Some other examples are:

tukang becak	rickshaw driver (not **pebecak**)
tukang ledeng	plumber (not **peledeng**)
tukang listrik	electrician (not **pelistrik**)

Here are some more words for which we can use **tukang**. Find out how to say them in Indonesian.

welder
photographer
carpenter
magican
hitman

Something having the function associated with the base word

BASE WORD	ENGLISH MEANING	PEN- NOUN	ENGLISH MEANING
buka	to open	**pembuka**	opener (for example, can opener)
dingin	cold	**pendingin**	cooler
garis	line	**penggaris**	ruler
hapus	to erase	**penghapus**	eraser, duster (for blackboards)
ikat	to tie	**pengikat**	instrument for tying
panas	hot	**pemanas**	heater
potong	to cut	**pemotong**	cutter
pukul	to hit	**pemukul**	instrument for hitting

Some other similar words simply mean 'something associated with the base word'.

BASE WORD	ENGLISH MEANING	PEN- NOUN	ENGLISH MEANING
sakit	sick	**penyakit**	sickness, illness
sebab	to cause	**penyebab**	cause

LATIHAN 2

The following are noun phrases containing **peN-** words. Find out what they mean in English. You may need to consult your dictionary for this exercise.

1 Hidangan pembuka
2 Pecandu musik techno

3 Pemakan daging
4 Pembuka kaleng
5 Pemungut sampah
6 Pendatang baru
7 Pendingin ruangan
8 Pemotong rumput
9 Penjual rokok
10 Penjaga toko
11 Pengikat rambut
12 Pencinta binatang

16.2 *PeN-* adjectives

Some **peN-** words are adjectives and they are derived from adjectival base words. The derived adjectives mean 'person having the characteristics described by the base word'.

BASE WORD	ENGLISH MEANING	PEN- ADJECTIVE	ENGLISH MEANING
diam	quiet	**pendiam**	quiet person
malas	lazy	**pemalas**	lazy person
malu	shy	**pemalu**	shy person
marah	angry	**pemarah**	person who is quick to anger
riang	cheerful	**periang**	cheerful person

LATIHAN 3

Work in pairs, taking turns to interview each other in Indonesian about the characteristics of five people you know well. You must use the adjectives in the above table in your description, preceded by the 'degree words' listed below. More than one adjective should be used for each description.

sedikit (a little)
tidak begitu (not so)
sangat (very)
paling (most)

Example:

Ayah saya: **sedikit pemalu dan sangat pendiam.**
My father: a little shy and very quiet.

LATIHAN 4

Give the **peN-** form of the following base words, then check the English meaning of each **peN-** word by consulting your dictionary.

BASE WORD	*PEN-* FORM	ENGLISH MEANING
1 salur		
2 bakar		
3 buru		
4 didik		
5 jilat		
6 samar		
7 culik		
8 samun		
9 selidik		
10 teliti		

Summary

- **PeN-** words are mostly nouns, but some are adjectives.
- They often have either corresponding **meN-** or **ber-** verbs.
- **PeN-** nouns mean either 'person' or 'thing' associated with the base word.
- **PeN-** adjectives describe the characteristics of a person.

17

-an

Like other affixes, the **-an** suffix has several functions, the main one being to form a noun. Its other functions are to form adjectives and adverbs.

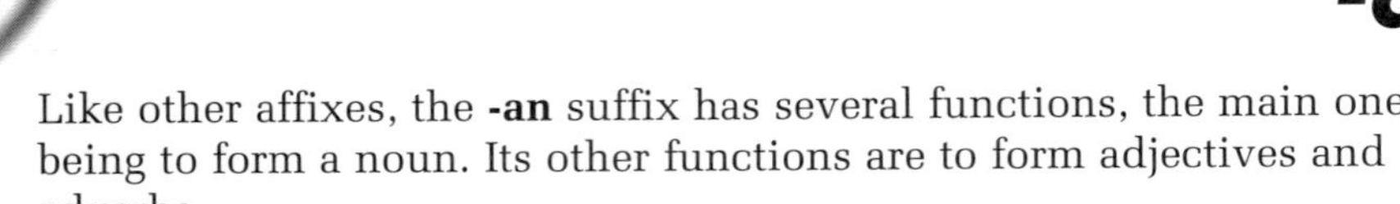

17.1 Forming a noun

Nouns with **-an** can be derived from verbs or adjectives.

BASE WORD	ENGLISH MEANING	-AN NOUN	ENGLISH MEANING
bantu	to help	**bantuan**	help, assistance, aid
bundar	round	**bundaran**	roundabout
gantung	to hang	**gantungan**	hanger
karang	to compose an essay	**karangan**	essay
keluh	to complain, sigh	**keluhan**	complaint
kenal	to know a person	**kenalan**	acquaintance
kotor	dirty	**kotoran**	dirt, excrement
main	to play	**mainan**	toy
makan	to eat	**makanan**	food
masuk	to go in, enter	**masukan**	input
minum	to drink	**minuman**	drink
parkir	to park	**parkiran**	parking lot

Modifying another noun

Words with the **-an** suffix can also be used in a noun phrase to modify another noun.

BASE WORD	ENGLISH MEANING	NOUN PHRASE	ENGLISH MEANING
beli	to buy	**barang belian**	purchased goods
curi	to steal	**barang curian**	stolen goods
pinjam	to borrow	**uang pinjaman**	borrowed money (debt)
sewa	to rent, hire	**rumah sewaan**	rented house

Reduplicated nouns

TO INDICATE VARIETY

NOUN	ENGLISH MEANING
buah-buahan	variety of fruit
bunga-bungaan	variety of flowers
daun-daunan	variety of leaves
obat-obatan	medication (variety of medicine)
sayur-sayuran	variety of vegetables
tumbuh-tumbuhan	variety of plants, flora

TO RESEMBLE WHAT IS INDICATED BY THE BASE WORD

In this group are words that can be nouns or verbs. The nouns usually refer to toy things, while the verbs refer to playing or pretending to do something.

NOUN	ENGLISH MEANING
kuda-kudaan	rocking-horse
mobil-mobilan	toy car
orang-orangan	toy person (for example, scarecrow)
rumah-rumahan	toy house
(main) koboi-koboian	to play cowboys
masak-masakan	to pretend to cook
sembunyi-sembunyian	to play hide-and-seek

LATIHAN 1

Below are some base words and their meaning in English. Form a noun from each by adding the suffix **-an**. Guess the meaning in English of each **-an** noun, then check your dictionary to see if your guess is correct.

	BASE WORD	ENGLISH MEANING	*-AN* NOUN	ENGLISH MEANING
1	**pukul**	to hit		
2	**pakai**	to wear		
3	**tulis**	to write		
4	**baca**	to read		
5	**tonton**	to watch		
6	**jual**	to sell		
7	**peluk**	to embrace		
8	**tanam**	to plant, sow		
9	**cicil**	to pay in instalments		
10	**tabrak**	to collide		

LATIHAN 2

Translate these noun phrases into English. You may need to consult your dictionary for this exercise.

1 Barang dagangan
2 Uang cicilan
3 Uang simpanan
4 Anak jalanan
5 Mobil sewaan
6 Baju pinjaman
7 Jam tangan curian
8 Warna celupan
9 Manajer bohongan
10 Pekerjaan borongan

LATIHAN 3

Translate these noun phrases into Indonesian.

1 Toy fish
2 Toy train
3 Toy calculator
4 Toy telephone
5 Toy computer

17.2 Forming an adjective

Adjectives with the suffix **-an** are derived from either another adjective or a noun.

BASE WORD	ENGLISH MEANING	-AN ADJECTIVE	ENGLISH MEANING
kampung	village	**kampungan**	country bumpkin (negative connotation)
murah	cheap	**murahan**	trashy, low quality

17.3 *-an* with numbers

When **-an** is attached to some numbers, it means 'in the multiplication of'.

BASE WORD	ENGLISH MEANING	-AN WORD	ENGLISH MEANING
ratus	hundred	**ratusan**	hundreds of
ribuan	thousand	**ribuan**	thousands of
juta	million	**jutaan**	millions of
miliar	billion	**miliaran**	billions of

When **-an** is attached to some fractional numbers, however, the meaning is quite different.

BASE WORD	ENGLISH MEANING	-AN WORD	ENGLISH MEANING
seperempat	one-quarter	**perempatan**	intersection
sepertiga	one-third	**pertigaan**	T-intersection
setengah	half	**pertengahan**	middle

17.4 Forming an adverb

Adverbs with the suffix **-an** are usually reduplicated.

BASE WORD	ENGLISH MEANING	-AN ADVERB	ENGLISH MEANING
besar	large	**besar-besaran**	on a large scale
habis	all gone	**habis-habisan**	exhaustively
kecil	small	**kecil-kecilan**	on a small scale
mati	to die, dead	**mati-matian**	with a lot of effort
terang	clear	**terang-terangan**	openly, frankly
untung	lucky	**untung-untungan**	with luck

LATIHAN 4

KOSAKATA

barang	goods
dirayakan	celebrated
kecelakaan	accident
memaki	to swear
membeli	to buy
menang	to win
rusak	broken
uang kas	cash
usaha	business

Complete each of the following sentences with a word from the box. Each word may be used only once.

pertengahan	mati-matian
kampungan	kecil-kecilan
perempatan	untung-untungan
besar-besaran	habis-habisan
terang-terangan	murahan

1 Dia berusaha ________________ untuk menang.
2 Joni dengan ________________ mencuri uang kas di toko itu.
3 Ulang tahun bapaknya yang ke-50 dirayakan ________________.
4 Dia memaki temannya ________________ kemarin.
5 Bu Yati membuka usaha ________________ di pasar.
6 Keluarga Burhan akan berlibur ke Adelaide pada ________________ tahun.
7 Jangan membeli barang ________________, nanti cepat rusak.
8 Kemarin terjadi kecelakaan di ________________ jalan itu.
9 Membeli tattslotto itu ________________; bisa menang, bisa tidak.
10 Lina tidak suka kepada Toni, karena Toni ________________.

Summary

- The majority of words with the **-an** suffix are nouns.
- Words with the **-an** suffix can also be verbs, adjectives or adverbs.
- Reduplicated **-an** words are either nouns or adverbs.

18

PeN–an and Per–an

Words with **peN–an** and **per–an** are mostly abstract nouns (things we cannot touch, see or feel). Many of these nouns come from verbs and, as such, they carry some element of 'action' in their meaning. This is rather different from many **ke–an** words which are also abstract nouns, but in which no 'action' is implied.

However, not all **peN–an** and **per–an** words come from verbs. Some are noun-based, which makes them more like **ke–an** nouns.

Because of their abstract nature, **peN–an** and **per–an** words are abundant in areas of language use where abstract concepts are required, such as newspaper and magazine articles, books, academic writing and talks about economic, historical, political and other issues.

18.1 PeN–an

Most **peN–an** words are derived from **meN-** verbs. This is why the sound changes in **meN-** verbs are also found in **peN–an** words.

MEN- VERB	ENGLISH MEANING	PEN–AN NOUN	ENGLISH MEANING
memakai	to use	**pemakaian**	use, usage
memandang	to gaze	**pemandangan**	scenery
membaca	to read	**pembacaan**	reading
membangun	to build	**pembangunan**	development
membeli	to buy, purchase	**pembelian**	purchase
membuat	to make	**pembuatan**	the making of
menanam	to plant	**penanaman**	the planting of
mencium	to smell, kiss, sniff	**penciuman**	sense of smell
mendengar	to hear	**pendengaran**	sense of hearing
menginap	to stay the night	**penginapan**	inn, motel
mengirim	to send	**pengiriman**	the sending of, dispatch
menjual	to sell	**penjualan**	the selling of, sale
menulis	to write	**penulisan**	the writing of
menyeberang	to cross (for example, street)	**penyeberangan**	crossing

MeN–kan and *meN–i*

Some **peN–an** nouns also come from **meN–kan** or **meN–i** words.

MEN–I OR MEN–KAN VERB	ENGLISH MEANING	PEN–AN NOUN	ENGLISH MEANING
membicarakan	to talk about	**pembicaraan**	talk, discussion
menduduki	to occupy	**pendudukan**	occupation
menemukan	to find	**penemuan**	finding, discovery
menerjemahkan	to translate	**penerjemahan**	the translating of, translation
mengetahui	to know	**pengetahuan**	knowledge
menggunakan	to use	**penggunaan**	use, usage

18.2 *Per–an*

Many **per–an** nouns come from **ber-** verbs and, therefore, like their **peN–an** counterparts, most of them have an element of 'action' in their meaning. There are no sound changes involved with **per–an** nouns.

BER- VERB	ENGLISH MEANING	PER–AN NOUN	ENGLISH MEANING
berbeda	to differ	**perbedaan**	difference
berbuat	to do, commit	**perbuatan**	act, behaviour
berdagang	to trade, do business	**perdagangan**	trade
berjalan	to walk	**perjalanan**	trip
bertanding	to compete	**pertandingan**	competition
bertani	to farm	**pertanian**	farming
bertemu	to meet	**pertemuan**	meeting

Note

The consonant **'r'** in the prefix **ber-** disappears when attached to the base word **kerja**. The **per–an** noun derived from this verb follows the same pattern; thus **pekerjaan**, not **perkerjaan**.

BER- + KERJA	ENGLISH MEANING	PER–AN NOUN	ENGLISH MEANING
bekerja	to work	**pekerjaan**	work, job

In some cases, words having the same base word can be transformed into either **meN–(kan/i)** or **ber-** verbs, and from these verbs we can get either **peN–an** or **per–an** abstract nouns. Each affixation results in a different meaning.

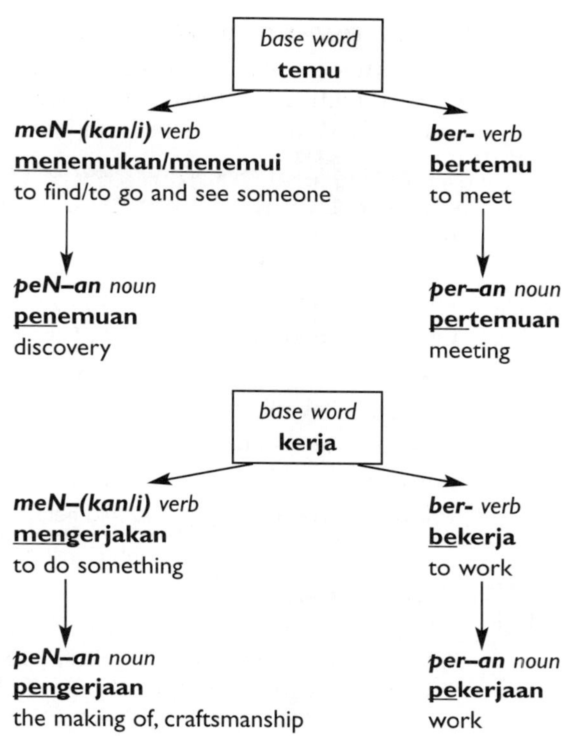

LATIHAN 1

Each of the following incomplete sentences contains a **meN-**, **meN–kan**, **meN–i** or **ber-** verb. Complete each sentence using a **peN–an** or **per–an** abstract noun.

KOSAKATA

awal	beginning
bagian	a part
berguna	useful
berjudul	entitled
jenis	variety
masa	period
melawan	against
menteri	minister
musim hujan	rainy season
umat manusia	mankind

1. Tempat orang menginap namanya ____________________.
2. Para menteri akan bertemu sore ini. ____________________ mereka adalah yang pertama kali.
3. Petenis dari Amerika itu akan bertanding melawan petenis Australia. ____________________ itu adalah bagian dari Australian Open.
4. Louis Pasteur adalah orang yang pertama kali menemukan obat anti anthrax dan rabies. ____________________nya sangat berguna bagi umat manusia.
5. Para petani akan menanam padi jenis baru tahun ini. ____________________ nya akan dimulai pada awal musim hujan nanti.
6. Jepang menduduki Indonesia tahun 1942–45. Masa ____________________ itu pendek.
7. Garin Nugroho membuat film seri yang berjudul 'Anak Seribu Pulau'. ____________________ film seri itu memakan waktu lama.
8. Umar Kayam menulis novel yang berjudul 'Para Priyayi'. ____________________ novel itu dilakukannya di Amerika dan Indonesia.

Other *per–an* nouns

Some other **per–an** nouns are rather irregular in the sense that they are not systematically derived from **ber-** verbs. The following are either from **meN–(kan/i)** verbs or from base words.

BASE WORD	**MEN–(KAN/I)** VERB	ENGLISH MEANING	**PER–AN** NOUN	ENGLISH MEANING
bintang		star	**perbintangan**	astrology, astronomy
coba	**mencoba**	to try	**percobaan**	experiment
film	**memfilm**	to film	**perfilman**	film industry
kota		city	**perkotaan**	city areas
nikah	**menikah**	to get married	**pernikahan**	wedding
pinta	**meminta**	to request	**permintaan**	request, demand
pustaka		reading	**perpustakaan**	library
tolong	**menolong**	to help	**pertolongan**	help, assistance

Did you know?
The word for 'tertiary institution' or 'higher education' (which really is the same as 'university') in Indonesian is also a **per–an** word: **perguruan tinggi.**

18.3 *Pe–an*

Some other abstract nouns are prefixed by **pe-** rather than **peN-** or **per-**, unlike the ones we previously encountered. These nouns have irregular bases: some are from base words; some are from **meN–kan**; some are from **ber-**.

BASE WORD	**MEN–KAN** OR **BER-** WORD	ENGLISH MEANING	**PE–AN** NOUN	ENGLISH MEANING
gunung		mountain	**pegunungan**	mountainous/hilly areas
desa		village	**pedesaan**	village/country areas
gadai	**menggadaikan**	to pawn	**pegadaian**	pawnshop
kubur	**menguburkan**	to bury	**pekuburan**	graveyard
mukim	**bermukim**	to settle	**pemukiman**	settlement

LATIHAN 2

The following table contains some Indonesian verbs with their English meaning. Write the abstract noun form of each verb and guess its English meaning. Check your answers in the dictionary. The first one is done for you.

VERB	ENGLISH MEANING	ABSTRACT NOUN	ENGLISH MEANING
1 **mengalami**	to experience	**pengalaman**	experience
2 **merawat**	to care for		
3 **mengobati**	to treat medically		
4 **berkembang**	to develop		
5 **memahami**	to comprehend		
6 **membuka**	to open		
7 **menutup**	to close		
8 **menderita**	to suffer		
9 **memeriksa**	to check, inspect		
10 **menata**	to arrange		

LATIHAN 3

Listed below on the left are some noun phrases pertaining to beauty and skin care found in various Indonesian magazines. Match them with their English counterparts on the right.

1 **Penataan rambut**	Premature aging
2 **Perawatan kecantikan**	Beauty care
3 **Penuaan dini**	Hair styling
4 **Peremajaan kulit**	Body slimming
5 **Pelangsingan tubuh**	Skin rejuvenation

LATIHAN 4

Below are some common phrases in English. Do you know how to say them in Indonesian? Use the **peN–an** or **per–an** prefix for the English words ending with '-ing'. You may need to consult your dictionary for this exercise.

1 Bread making
2 Language teaching
3 Candle making
4 Poetry reading
5 House buying
6 Book publishing
7 Dictionary making
8 Book binding
9 Letter writing
10 Fund raising (in Indonesian, literally 'fund collecting')

Summary

- Most **peN–an** and **per–an** words are abstract nouns; some are concrete nouns.
- Most are derived from verbs and, as such, they contain an element of 'action' in their meaning. Some are from nouns, much like **ke–an** nouns.
- Many **peN–an** nouns come from **meN-**, **meN–kan** or **meN–i** verbs.
- Many **per–an** nouns are from **ber-** verbs. Some others are either from **meN-** verbs or from base words.
- **Pe–an** nouns are from either **meN-** or **ber-** verbs or from base words.

19

Subject-focus and Object-focus

The terms *subject-focus* and *object-focus* are so called because in these sentence constructions our attention is focused on the subject or the object of the sentence. You will find that they are also called *active voice* and *passive voice* in other grammar books.

A *subject* is, generally speaking, a doer, actor or *agent* of an action.

An *object* is, on the other hand, someone or something that is affected by the action performed by the subject.

For example, if my dog ate a cake that I have just baked, the cake is the object (it is 'affected' by the action of eating) and the dog is the subject (that does the eating).

In effect, then, the subject-focus and the object-focus constructions are really about what it is in the sentence that becomes our focus of attention. Whatever gets the focus, comes first in the sentence. If the focus is on the subject, the subject comes first in the sentence; if the focus is on the object, the object comes first.

19.1 Subject-focus

The subject-focus construction can be identified by the following.

1. The subject comes before the verb and the object.
2. The subject is followed by a **meN-**, **meN–kan** or **meN–i** transitive verb.
3. There may be an auxiliary verb before the **meN-** verb (see below).
4. The object follows the verb directly, with nothing preceding it (for example, a preposition).

In short, a simple subject-focus sentence consists of:

SUBJECT – TRANSITIVE VERB – OBJECT

Nina	**menulis**	**cerpen.**
Subject	*Verb*	*Object*
Nina	is writing	a short story.

Dokter	**memeriksa**	**pasien**
Subject	*Verb*	*Object*
The doctor	is examining	a patient.

To make our sentences a little more interesting, we can insert a few extra things, such as auxiliary verbs, adverbs and prepositional phrases (see earlier chapters for prepositional phrases).

Auxiliary verbs

Auxiliary verbs are words that are complementary to the main verb. In the sentence, they appear before the main verb. Auxiliaries express such things as *aspect* and *modality*. Aspect indicates whether an action is in the process, completed or not completed, or will be completed. Modality expresses such things as uncertainty, possibility or necessity.

ASPECT	ENGLISH MEANING	MODALITY	ENGLISH MEANING
sedang	in process of	**barangkali**	maybe, probably, possibly
belum	not yet	**bisa**	can, be able to
sudah	already	**boleh**	may
akan	will, be going to	**dapat**	can, be able to
		harus	must, have to
		ingin	want, wish to, will
		mau	want, wish to, will
		mungkin	maybe, probably, possibly

Adverbs

Adverbs are words that indicate such things as *frequency*, *manner* and *time*. They can be inserted either at the beginning or at the end of the sentence.

INDICATION	ADVERB	ENGLISH MEANING
Frequency	**lima kali seminggu**	five times a week
Manner	**pelan-pelan**	slowly
Time	**pagi ini**	this morning

Let us now see how we can incorporate auxiliary verbs, adverbs and prepositional phrases into our subject-focus construction.

Nina	**akan**	**menulis**	**cerpen**	**besok.**
Subject	*Auxiliary verb*	*Main verb*	*Object*	*Adverb (time)*
Nina	will	write	a short story	tomorrow.

Dokter	**sedang**	**memeriksa**	**pasien**	**di ruang 3.**
Subject	*Auxiliary verb*	*Main verb*	*Object*	*Prepositional phrase*
The doctor	is in the process of	examining	a patient	in Room 3.

You can also insert two auxiliary verbs before the main verb, one indicating aspect and the other indicating modality.

Nina	**barangkali**	**akan**	**menulis**	**cerpen**	**besok.**
Subject	*Auxiliary verb*	*Auxiliary verb*	*Main verb*	*Object*	*Adverb (time)*
Nina	will	probably	write	a short story	tomorrow.

LATIHAN 1

Now that you have learnt about the subject-focus construction, try to write your own sentences by copying and completing the following table.

	SUBJECT	AUXILIARY VERB	MAIN VERB	OBJECT	ADVERB OR PREPOSITIONAL PHRASE
1	Manajer bank itu				
2	Tetangga kami				
3			mengangkat		
4			mengundang		
5		sedang			
6		boleh			
7					dari perpustakaan
8					cepat-cepat
9				konser musik klasik	
10				uang saya	

KOSAKATA

cepat-cepat	quickly
konser	concert
manajer bank	bank manager
mengangkat	to lift
mengundang	to invite someone (for example, to a party)
perpustakaan	library
tetangga	neighbour
uang	money

19.2 Object-focus

As mentioned, in an object-focus sentence our attention is focused on the object of the sentence. This is often difficult for English speakers, because in English we tend to focus on the subject. An additional difficulty in learning this construction comes from the fact that many object-focus sentences in Indonesian do not have exact equivalents in English. Many such sentences would have to be translated into subject-focus in English to be acceptable.

The object-focus construction is important to learn, simply because it is so prevalent in spoken and written Indonesian. The steps given below are to guide you in forming object-focus sentences.

Step 1

Identify whether the *subject* is the first, second or third person.

FIRST PERSON (SPEAKER OR PEOPLE REPRESENTED BY THE SPEAKER)

Singular:	Pronouns: **saya**, **aku**, **-ku**
Plural:	Pronouns: **kami**, **kita**

SECOND PERSON (PERSON SPOKEN TO: THE ADDRESSEE)

Singular:	Pronouns: **kamu**, **engkau**, **kau**, **anda**
	Address terms: for example, **Bapak**, **Ibu**, **Saudara**
Plural:	Pronouns: **kamu**, **kalian**, **anda sekalian**, **Saudara sekalian**

THIRD PERSON (PERSON OR THING SPOKEN ABOUT)

Singular:	Pronouns: **dia**, **-nya**
	Proper names: for example, **Tommy**, **Mira**, **Pak Hamid**
	Other noun phrases: for example, **kucing itu**, **murid itu**
Plural:	Pronoun: **mereka**
	Proper names: for example, **Tommy dan Mira**
	Other noun phrases: for example, **kucing-kucing itu**, **murid-murid itu**

Step 2

If the subject is the first or second person, the order is:

OBJECT – SUBJECT – VERB (no prefix, but retain suffix if there)

If the subject is the third person, there are two variations.

VARIATION A

If the subject is either a pronoun (for example, **dia**, **mereka**) or a proper name (for example, **Bu Rani**, **guru-guru itu**, **para sopir bis**), the order is:

OBJECT – VERB (with ***di-*** prefix and suffix, if there) **– (*OLEH*) SUBJECT**

Note

The word **oleh** (by), is optional. When it is followed by the pronoun **dia**, this pronoun is shortened into **-nya**.

oleh dia → **olehnya**

When speaking informally, people often prefer the word **sama** to **oleh**.

Baju saya	**dicuci**	**<u>sama</u>**	**dia.**
Object	*Verb*	*by*	*Subject*
My shirt	was washed	<u>by</u>	him.

→ He washed my shirt.

VARIATION B

If the subject is a pronoun, you can follow the same order as for first and second persons. We cannot do this if the subject is a proper name (for example, **Pak Hamid**) or a noun phrase (for example, **kucing itu**).

Summary of the rules

SUBJECT	RULE
First or second person	**Object – Subject – Verb** (no prefix on verb; suffix retained)
Third person (pronoun or proper name)	**Object – Verb – (oleh) Subject** (prefix **di-** on verb; suffix retained)
Third person (pronoun only)	**Object – Subject – Verb** (no prefix on verb; suffix retained)

19.3 Transforming subject-focus into object-focus

Now we will see how the rules for subject-focus and object-focus sentences can be applied to sentences.

First or second person subject

SUBJECT-FOCUS

SUBJECT	VERB (TRANSITIVE **MEN-**)	OBJECT
Saya **Kami** **Kita**	**membuat**	**kue coklat.**
Anda **Kamu** **Saudara** **(Eng)kau**	**membuat**	**kue coklat**

OBJECT-FOCUS

OBJECT	SUBJECT	VERB (NO PREFIX)
Kue coklat	**saya** **kami** **kita**	**buat**
Kue coklat	**Anda** **Kamu** **Saudara** **(Eng)kau**	**buat**

Third person subject

SUBJECT-FOCUS

SUBJECT	VERB (TRANSITIVE **MEN-**)	OBJECT
Dia	**membuat**	**kue coklat**
Mereka		
Pak Burhan	**membuat**	**kue coklat**
Bu Made		
Guru-guru itu		

OBJECT-FOCUS

Variation A: Subject is either pronoun or proper name

OBJECT	VERB (**DI-** PREFIX)	**(OLEH)** SUBJECT
Kue coklat	**dibuat**	**olehnya, -nya**
		(oleh) mereka
Kue coklat	**dibuat**	**(oleh) Pak Burhan**
		(oleh) Bu Made
		(oleh) guru-guru itu

Variation B: Subject is pronoun only

OBJECT	SUBJECT	VERB (NO PREFIX)
Kue coklat	**dia**	**buat**
	mereka	

LATIHAN 2

The following are simple subject-focus sentences with either first, second or third person subject. Transform them into object-focus sentences as shown above.

KOSAKATA

kuliah lecture
melempari to throw something at (repeatedly)
memenangkan to win
mencari to look for
mengikuti ujian to sit an exam
sayembara competition

First person subject

1 Saya	membaca	novel.
2 Kami	menonton	televisi.
3 Kita	menyanyikan	sebuah lagu.

Second person subject

4 Anda	menjual	pakaian.
5 Kamu	mengambil	koran.
6 Saudara	mendengarkan	kuliah.

Third person subject

7 Dia	mencari	pekerjaan.
8 Mereka	mengikuti	ujian.
9 Anita	memenangkan	sayembara.
10 Anak-anak	melempari	pohon.

Object-focus with auxiliary, prepositional phrase and adverb

We saw earlier that simple subject-focus constructions consisting of Subject – Verb – Object can be made more interesting by adding auxiliary verbs, prepositional phrases and adverbs. These constructions can be transformed into object-focus constructions. The simplest way to do this is by following the above rules, while leaving these additional things where they are. That is to say, we do not need to move them around or make any other changes the way we do with the subject, verb and object.

SUBJECT-FOCUS

Nina	**akan**	**menulis**	**cerpen**	**besok.**
Subject	*Auxiliary verb*	*Main verb*	*Object*	*Adverb of time*

OBJECT-FOCUS

Cerpen	**akan**	**ditulis**	**Nina**	**besok**
Object	*Auxiliary verb*	*Main verb*	*Subject*	*Adverb of time*

SUBJECT-FOCUS

Dokter	**sedang**	**memeriksa**	**pasien**	**di ruang 3.**
Subject	*Auxiliary verb*	*Main verb*	*Object*	*Prepositional phrase*

OBJECT-FOCUS

Pasien	**sedang**	**diperiksa**	**dokter**	**di ruang 3.**
Object	*Auxiliary verb*	*Main verb*	*Subject*	*Prepositional phrase*

LATIHAN 3

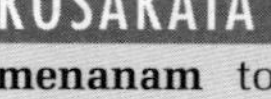

menanam to plant
mengantarkan to take someone/something somewhere
mengunjungi to visit

Transform the sentences below into object-focus constructions. Remember to keep the auxiliary verb, prepositional phrase and the adverb where they are in each sentence.

1	Kami	akan	mengunjungi	keluarga Burhan	bulan depan.
2	Istrinya	sedang	mengantarkan	anak mereka	ke dokter.
3	Anda	boleh	menonton	program itu	besok
4	Bu Tirta	akan	menjual	pisang	di pasar
5	Saya	ingin	menanam	pohon apel	di kebun saya

LATIHAN 4

Write an object-focus sentence, using the auxiliary **akan**, to describe what is happening or what will or may happen to each of the objects shown below. Remember that you must use a transitive verb for this. Start your sentences with the words provided.

Example:

Bunga ini ...

Bunga ini akan saya beli.

Literally: This flower I will buy → I will buy this flower.

1 Kotak emas itu ...
2 Siswa dari Indonesia iu ...
3 Telephon genggam ini ...
4 Tugas itu ...
5 Tiket pesawat terbang ini ....

Questions in object-focus using *apa yang* and *siapa yang*

The object-focus construction can also be used in interrogative sentences. Rather than asking a question in subject-focus, we can use an object-focus construction starting with **Apa yang ...?** (What is it that ...?) if the object is inanimate, or **Siapa yang ...?** (Who is it that ...?) if the object is a person. In the following examples, the object is underlined.

FIRST PERSON SUBJECT

Statement:	**Saya memasak <u>nasi</u>.**
Question in subject-focus:	**Saya memasak <u>apa</u>?**
Question in object-focus:	**<u>Apa yang</u> saya masak?**

SECOND PERSON SUBJECT

Statement:	**Saudara akan membeli <u>mobil</u>.**
Question in subject-focus:	**Saudara akan membeli <u>apa</u>?**
Question in object-focus:	**<u>Apa yang</u> akan Saudara beli?**

THIRD PERSON SUBJECT

Statement:	**Mereka menelepon <u>teman saya</u>.**
Question in subject-focus:	**Mereka menelepon <u>siapa</u>?**
Question in object-focus:	**<u>Siapa yang</u> mereka telpon?**
	<u>Siapa yang</u> ditelepon (oleh) mereka?

LATIHAN 5

Turn the following statements into object-focus questions by using either **Apa yang ...?** or **Siapa yang ...?**. The object in each sentence is underlined.

1 Kami makan <u>nasi</u> setiap hari.
2 Bu Siti membawa <u>keranjang</u>.
3 Mereka membuat <u>majalah dinding sekolah</u>.
4 Saya akan menelepon <u>Toni</u>.
5 Anda akan menerima <u>hadia besar</u>.

KOSAKATA

keranjang	basket
menerima	to receive
menyuruh	to ask somebody to do something
pulang	to go home
tukang becak	rickshaw driver

6 Pak Totok menjual buah-buahan di pasar.
7 Rita dan Dani memanggil tukang becak itu.
8 Saya suka menonton film horor.
9 Guru menyuruh murid-murid pulang.
10 Anak-anak mencuri mangga di kebun Bu Rini.

Object-focus with unmentioned subject

Many object-focus sentences appear without the subject. This is because the subject is either known, assumed, non-specific (for example, someone, something) or not so important as to warrant a mention.

Mobil saya	**dicuri.**
Object	*Verb*
My car	was stolen.

In this example, we know that someone stole the car, but the person is not identified. What is important in this sentence is the fact that the car was stolen, not so much who stole it.

Object-focus with no subject usually takes the **di-** form (third person, Variation A) and is often found in news reports and advertisements. Here are some real examples from Indonesian newspapers.

News headlines:

500 orang dikabarkan tewas dalam gempa bumi itu.
500 people are reported dead in that earthquake.

Penjahat mati didor di angkutan umum
Criminal shot dead in public transport

Classified advertisements:

Rumah dijual
Literally: House to be sold → House for sale

Mobil dijual
Literally: Car to be sold → Car for sale

LATIHAN 6

Below are some titles of classified advertisements and some news headlines from Indonesian newspapers. Find out what they mean in English. You may need to consult your dictionary for this exercise.

Classified advertisements:
1 Rumah dikontrakkan
2 Tanah dijual
3 Toko disewakan
4 Mobil dicari

News headlines:
5 Penculik anak divonis 18 bulan
6 31 Truk kayu ilegal ditangkap
7 Anak perwira digebuki

8 Penyelundup narkoba diperiksa Rabu
9 Penduduk dipersenjatai dan disebar
10 Pemilik toko mati ditusuk

LATIHAN 7

Here are descriptions of two Indonesian spices—**pala** (nutmeg) and **kemiri** (candle nuts) — containing object-focus sentences, from the recipe book *Masakan Indonesia*. Both of these spices are used widely in Indonesian cooking. Translate the descriptions into English. You may need to consult your dictionary for this exercise.

Pala dan Bunga Pala

Biji pala dibungkus kulit yang keras dan dibalut oleh bunga pala yang menyerupai jala kemerahan. Bunga maupun bijinya dikeringkan. Aroma bunga lebih halus dari pada biji, dibeli dan dipakai secara utuh atau dihaluskan.

Kemiri

Bentuk bulat dan berwarna kuning muda, rasanya gurih. Sebelum digunakan sebaiknya disangrai atau digoreng lebih dulu supaya bau langu dan racunnya hilang. Kemiri dapat digantikan oleh Macadamia yang tumbuh di Hawai (harganya cukup mahal). Kacang mete goreng atau kenari juga bisa digunakan sebagai pengganti.

Yasa Boga, *Masakan Indonesia*, PT Gramedia Pustaka Utama, 1997, p. 17

LATIHAN 8

Look at each of the following two sets of pictures. Picture B shows that some things have been done to the objects in Picture A. Work in pairs to ask and answer questions in Indonesian about the pictures before and after the changes. Use the **di-** object-focus construction for the answers.

Example:

A: Bagaimana roti ini?
How's this bread?

B: Belum diiris.
Not yet sliced.

or

Sudah diiris.
Already sliced.

1 Picture A

Picture B

2 Picture A

Picture B

Summary

- Subject-focus and object-focus are about what it is in the sentence that becomes the focus of our attention.
- Simple subject-focus consists of: Subject – Transitive verb – Object.
- We can add auxiliary verbs, prepositional phrases and adverbs to the sentence to make it more interesting.
- To transform subject-focus into object-focus, determine first whether the subject is first, second or third person, then follow the rules:

—First person:	Object – Subject – Verb
—Second person:	Object – Subject – Verb
—Third person:	Object – **di-** Verb – (**oleh**) Subject
	Object – Subject – Verb (if subject is pronoun)

- Remember that it is only the third person that gets the **di-** form.
- Many object-focus sentences do not have a subject. This is because the subject is known by context, assumed, non-specific or not very important.

20

Uses of *-nya*

In this chapter we will learn about **-nya** in examples like these:

> **Anjingnya bernama Jack.**
> **Bagusnya!**
> **Airnya panas!**

The suffix **-nya** appears very often in spoken and written Indonesian. To make sense, **-nya** has to be attached to another word, which can be a noun, an adjective or a verb.

20.1 To show possession

When attached to a noun or noun phrase, **-nya** can indicate something that belongs to a third person (which, in spite of its name, can include things that are not people).

The suffix **-nya** is equivalent to the English 'his', 'her/hers' or 'its'; for example, 'her dog', 'his house', 'its tail'.

In this function, **-nya** replaces the pronoun **dia**, proper name referring to the third person or any noun phrase indicating a person, as shown in the following examples.

Ini buku dia	→	**Ini bukunya.**
Itu kantor Bu Tini	→	**Itu kantornya.**
Ini kamar anak saya	→	**Ini kamarnya.**

20.2 As equivalent of 'the'

The suffix **-nya** can also function as a *definite article*; that is, it can be used to refer to something already known or understood from context. In English, this is shown by the word 'the'.

Hawanya panas sekali hari ini.
The weather is very hot today.

Jangan lupa mengembalikan bukunya ya.
Don't forget to return the book, will you?

Ayo, bersihkan mobilnya.
Come on, clean the car.

Silakan makan kuenya!
Please eat the cake!

20.3 Exclamation

We can also attach **-nya** to an adjective to make an exclamatory remark about something. In a sentence, this exclamation usually comes before the noun or noun phrase that we exclaim about. For example, if we want to say how beautiful a flower is, then the word 'beautiful' comes first and 'flower' follows.

Cantiknya	**bunga ini!**
Adjective + nya	*Noun phrase*
How beautiful	this flower is!

Sulitnya	**ujian itu!**
Adjective + nya	*Noun phrase*
How difficult	the exam was!

Nakalnya	**anak ini!**
Adjective + nya	*Noun phrase*
How naughty	this child is!

We can, of course, use an exclamation to pay someone a compliment or to express surprise, exasperation, a sense of wonder and so on. Often people do not bother to mention the noun phrase because what they are exclaiming about is understood from context.

Enaknya!
How delicious! (for example, referring to food)

Dinginnya!
So cold! (for example, referring to the weather)

We can also add another exclamatory word, such as **aduh**, **wah** or **ampun**, in front of the adjective to give the exclamation more force.

Aduh, pelitnya!
My goodness, how scungy!

Wah, baunya!
Literally: Wow, the smell! (for example, referring to fragrant or bad smell)
→ Wow, the smells nice! *or* Oh, that stinks!

Ampun, nakalnya!
My goodness, so naughty! (for example, referring to a child's behaviour)

LATIHAN 1

Make up an exclamatory expression using **-nya** for each of the following situations. Add an exclamatory word in front of your adjective to reinforce it. You can mention the noun phrase after the adjective, if you wish. The adjectives are underlined to help you.

1 It is sweltering today. What might you say to your friend?
2 You see images of starving children on television and are struck by how thin the children are. What might you say?
3 You want to buy a handbag, but when you start looking in shops, you find that handbags are more expensive than you had expected. What might you say?
4 You go to your friend's dinner party, which you thought would be attended by a few people. When you arrive, you find that there are many more people than you had anticipated. What would you say?
5 When you are strolling down the street near your house one evening, you see a very tall tree that you never noticed before. You are struck by how tall the tree is. What would you say?

Here are some common exclamatory expressions in Indonesian. Give their equivalents in English. You may need to consult your dictionary for this exercise.

6 Aduh, lucunya boneka itu!
7 Wah, tebalnya buku ini!
8 Ampun, kerasnya musik itu!
9 Ampun, dinginnya hari ini!
10 Aduh, canggihnya teknologi baru itu!

20.4 To be polite

In many instances, Indonesian speakers avoid saying 'you' or 'your' to the person to whom they are speaking, out of politeness. Instead, **-nya** is often preferred, which may seem strange to English speakers, since it sounds like they are referring to something belonging to someone else. For instance, a very common way of asking 'What is your name?' is **Siapa namanya?**, which literally means 'What is the name?'. Likewise, to ask how old someone is, **-nya** is commonly used: **Berapa umurnya?**

Boleh saya pinjam bukunya?
Literally: May I borrow the book?
→ May I borrow your book?

Mobilnya bagus sekali!
Literally: The car is very beautiful!
→ Your car is very beautiful!

Sepatunya dibeli di mana?
Literally: The shoes, where were they bought?
→ Where did you buy your shoes?

LATIHAN 2

The following are things that people often say or ask in English. Translate them into Indonesian, using **-nya** to be polite. You may need to consult your dictionary for this exercise.

1 I really like your house.
2 Where is your car?
3 When is your exam?
4 What is your mother's name?
5 How old is your dog?
6 What is your occupation?
7 Your drawing is beautiful.
8 Your watch is slow.
9 What is your problem?
10 Where did you buy your shoes?

LATIHAN 3

Interview three of your friends in Indonesian, asking the following questions with **-nya**. Record their responses in a table as shown.

KOSAKATA

hari ulang tahun birthday
kesukaan favourite
saudara sibling

PERTANYAAN	TEMAN 1	TEMAN 2	TEMAN 3
1 Maaf, siapa namanya?			
2 Di mana tinggalnya?			
3 Kapan hari ulang tahunnya?			
4 Siapa nama ibunya?			
5 Siapa nama bapaknya?			
6 Ada berapa saudaranya?			
7 Siapa nama saudara-saudaranya?			
8 Apa makanan kesukaannya?			
9 Berapa nomer teleponnya?			
10 Hobinya apa?			

20.5 In topic–comment sentences

Topic–comment sentences are those in which the subject is the *topic* of the sentence (what the sentence is about) and it comes first, while what follows is the *comment* about that topic. In speech, there is usually a short pause between the topic and the comment. This is not so evident in writing.

Bu Rita **anaknya lima.**
Topic *Comment*
Literally: (As for) Bu Rita, her children are five.
→ Bu Rita has five children.

The suffix **-nya** is attached to the noun or noun phrase that belongs to the topic. In the example above, the children belong to Bu Rita; therefore, **-nya** is attached to **anak**.

Sekolah kami **perpustakaannya besar.**
Topic *Comment*
Literally: (As for) our school, its library is big.
→ Our school has a big library.

Teman saya — **jaket<u>nya</u> merah.**
Topic — *Comment*
Literally: (As for) my friend, <u>his/her</u> jacket is red.
→ My friend is wearing a red jacket.

LATIHAN 4

Match each of the topics in the left column with the comment in the right column.

KOSAKATA	
becak	rickshaw
harum	fragrant
jumlah	total number
mangkuk	bowl
penyiar	broadcaster
piring	plate
roda	wheel

1 CD saya	**a** baunya harum
2 Piring dan mangkuk ibu saya	**b** rodanya tiga
3 Roti dari toko itu	**c** jumlahnya banyak
4 Universitas itu	**d** penduduknya banyak sekali
5 Program televisi itu	**e** mahasiswanya banyak
6 Bapak teman saya	**f** namanya 'Sesame Street'
7 Indonesia	**g** warnanya putih
8 Becak	**h** namanya James
9 Bunga itu	**i** mobilnya Mazda
10 Penyiar radio itu	**j** rasanya enak

LATIHAN 5

Write a topic–comment sentence in Indonesian on each of the following topics. You may need to consult your dictionary for this exercise.

1 Their computer
2 My teacher's table
3 Her hat
4 That tree
5 That giraffe

20.6 To form abstract nouns

When attached to a verb or adjective **-nya** turns the word into an abstract noun. This is why in this function **-nya** is called a *nominaliser*. The process of forming the abstract noun is called *nominalisation*. In the following example, the verb **ditutup** (to be closed, shut down) in sentence **a** is turned into the noun **ditutupnya** (the closure of) in sentence **b**.

a **Bank itu <u>ditutup</u> oleh pemerintah bulan lalu.**
That bank was <u>shut down</u> by the government last month.

b **<u>Ditutupnya</u> bank itu menyebabkan kemarahan banyak orang.**
The <u>closure</u> of that bank caused anger in a lot of people.

Here are more examples of nominalisation of verbs.

a **Pembunuhan itu <u>terjadi</u> kemarin sore.**
That murder <u>happened</u> yesterday afternoon.

b **Terjadinya pembunuhan itu membuat polisi sibuk.**
The taking place of (occurrence) of that murder made the police busy.

a **Bapak saya pergi ke Mekah untuk naik haji.**
My father went to Mecca for a pilgrimage.

b **Perginya bapak saya ke Mekah adalah untuk naik haji.**
The departure of my father to Mecca is for a pilgrimage.

Here are some examples of nominalisation of adjectives.

a **Penghasilan mereka besar.**
Their income is high (literally 'large').

b **Besarnya penghasilan mereka memungkinkan mereka untuk membeli rumah mahal.**
The high level (literally 'the largeness') of their income enabled them to buy an expensive house.

LATIHAN 6

Turn the underlined verbs and adjectives in each of the following sentences into abstract nouns by writing a new sentence with similar information, using the nominalised word at the beginning of your sentence.

Example:

Swalayan itu dibuka 24 jam.
The supermarket is open twenty-four hours.
Dibukanya swalayan itu 24 jam membuat orang senang berbelanja di sana.
The opening of the supermarket for twenty-four hours makes people enjoy shopping there.

1 Sekolah itu dibuka oleh Menteri Pendidikan.
Dibukanya ...
2 Banyak orang hadir di pertemuan itu.
Hadirnya ...
3 Ribuan orang terbunuh dalam insiden berdarah itu.
Terbunuhnya ...
4 Target penjualan bulan ini sudah tercapai.
Tercapainya ...
5 Ruangan itu sangat besar.
Besarnya ...

Summary

The suffix **-nya** has several uses:

- To show possession ('his', 'her/hers' or 'its')
- In topic–comment sentences, attached to the word in the comment part
- As a definite article, like 'the' in English
- As an exclamatory marker: 'How ...!' 'What a/an ...!'
- As a nominaliser: to form an abstract noun from a verb or adjective
- To be polite by avoiding saying 'you' or 'your'

21

Ways to Say 'Because'

In this chapter we look at five ways to say 'because' in Indonesian.

- **(oleh) karena**
- **(oleh) sebab**
- **gara-gara**
- **mentang-mentang**
- **lantaran**

You may wonder why there are so many words to express the same thing. The answer is, although all of those words mean 'because', they differ in terms of:

- where they can occur in a sentence
- where they come from
- their degree of formality

Remember that English also has different words, such as 'because', 'for' and 'since'.

> He failed the test <u>because</u> he studied the wrong chapters.
> They didn't do it <u>for</u> fear of hurting her.
> I didn't include you <u>since</u> you didn't say anything.

Let us now look at the Indonesian words in turn.

21.1 *(Oleh) karena*

Karena is neutral in terms of formality, so it is suitable for any situation. However, sometimes people add **oleh** in front of it. When they do that, the expression sounds a little more formal.

Karena can be placed either at the beginning or middle of a sentence.

> **Adik saya tidak mau makan <u>karena</u> mulutnya sakit.**
> My younger brother/sister doesn't want to eat <u>because</u> his/her mouth is sore.

> **<u>Karena</u> gaji mereka tidak dinaikkan, para pekerja pabrik itu marah.**
> <u>Because</u> their wage was not increased, the workers of that factory were angry.

To say 'because of that', simply add **itu** after **karena**.

Tahun lalu terjadi gempa bumi di sana, (oleh) karena itu banyak orang tewas.
Last year there was an earthquake there; because of that many people died.

21.2 (Oleh) sebab

Sebab is also neutral in terms of formality and is often preceded by **oleh** (which is written in parentheses below to show that it is optional). The use of **oleh** makes the expression a little more formal.

Sebab cannot appear at the beginning of a sentence.

Saya membawa payung sebab kelihatannya akan hujan.
I'm carrying an umbrella because it looks like (it) will rain.

Toko-toko mulai memberikan diskon sebab hari Natal sudah dekat.
Shops begin to give discounts because Christmas is coming.

We can also add **itu** in the same way we do with **karena**.

Bayi itu lahir prematur; (oleh) sebab itu dia harus tinggal di rumah sakit selama tiga bulan pertama.
The baby was born premature; because of that he/she had to stay at the hospital for the first three months.

21.3 Gara-gara

This word comes from the Javanese word **goro-goro**. **Gara-gara** means 'because' in the sense of 'as a result of'.

Gara-gara can be placed either at the beginning or in the middle of a sentence.

Gara-gara kamu, saya dimarahi bapak.
Literally: As a result of your doing, I was scolded by father.
→ Because of you, I was scolded by father.

Hutan itu terbakar gara-gara orang seenaknya membuang puntung rokok.
The forest was burnt down as a result of someone carelessly throwing away cigarette butts.

21.4 Mentang-mentang

This reduplicated word means 'just because'. However, unlike its translation in English, **mentang-mentang** has a negative connotation. It should be placed at the beginning of a sentence.

Mentang-mentang kaya, dia sombong.
Just because (he/she) is wealthy, he/she is arrogant.

<u>Mentang-mentang</u> merasa pintar, mahasiswa itu tidak mau belajar.
<u>Just because</u> (he/she) feels (he/she is) smart, that university student does not want to study.

21.5 *Lantaran*

This word is informal and is therefore inappropriate for use in formal situations; for example, with your teacher in class. You may wish to use it with your friends instead.

Lantaran can be placed either at the beginning or middle of a sentence.

<u>Lantaran</u> banyak PR (pekerjaan rumah), saya tidak bisa ke bioskop.
<u>Because</u> (I have) a lot of homework, I can't go to the movies.

Piring dan mangkuk pecah semua <u>lantaran</u> dia ceroboh.
Plates and bowls broke <u>because</u> he/she was careless.

LATIHAN 1

Complete the sentences below with the 'because' words above. Bear in mind whether the word can occur at the beginning or middle of a sentence (or both).

1 Pak Sabirin terkena kanker paru-paru ________________________ merokok terlalu banyak.
2 ________________________ bisnisnya bangkrut, pemilik toko itu tidak bisa membayar hutangnya.
3 Pencuri itu pingsan ________________________ dipukuli orang sekampung.
4 Ekonomi Indonesia memburuk ________________________ situasi politik yang tidak stabil.
5 Bu Khatijah menangis sedih ________________________ rumahnya kebanjiran.
6 ________________________ sudah punya pacar, sekarang teman saya tidak pernah menelepon lagi.
7 ________________________ ngebut, dia ditangkap polisi.
8 Tanaman itu subur ________________________ sering diberi pupuk kandang.
9 Anak itu menderita ruam-ruam pada punggungnya ________________________ cuaca yang sangat panas.
10 Budi muntah-muntah ________________________ keracunan makanan.

KOSAKATA

bangkrut	bankrupt
hutang	debt
keracunan	to be poisoned
memburuk	to become bad, worsen
menderita	to suffer (from)
muntah-muntah	to vomit
ngebut	to speed
pacar	girlfriend/ boyfriend
paru-paru	lungs
pingsan	unconscious
pupuk kandang	manure
ruam-ruam	rash
subur	fertile
terkena	to be struck by, to contract (disease/ illness)

LATIHAN 2

Write sentences using the appropriate 'because' words for the following situations. You may need to consult your dictionary for this exercise.

1 You are late to class because you got up late this morning. What do you say to your teacher?

2 You could not come to your friend's party because you had to work. What do you say to your friend?
3 Your father asks you why you have not washed your clothes. Say that you are simply lazy.
4 Your friend rings to ask why you did not turn up to play tennis yesterday. Apologise and tell her that you had to take your younger sister to the dentist.
5 You go to the supermarket to buy groceries. At the checkout you realise that you forgot to bring your wallet. What do you say to the checkout person?

Translate the following sentences into Indonesian using the 'because' words discussed in this chapter. To help you, the Indonesian equivalents of the underlined words are given in parentheses.

6 I was annoyed with him because he lost my calculator. (**menghilangkan**)
7 Mira missed the plane because her taxi came late. (**ketinggalan**)
8 Because of you, our Maths teacher was angry with me. (**marah**)
9 Because of the prolonged conflict in that region, many people died. (**berkepanjangan**)
10 Just because you have money, you cannot treat other people like that. (**memperlakukan**)

LATIHAN 3

Work in pairs. Prepare five questions related to what you know about your partner's likes and dislikes or about what he or she wears or uses. Start your questions with **mengapa** (why)—or **kenapa**, if you want to be informal. Take turns interviewing each other.

Example:

> **Mengapa kamu suka apel?**
> Why do you like apples?
> **Karena menyehatkan dan rasanya enak.**
> Because (they are) healthy and taste good.

Summary

Ways of saying 'because':

- **(Oleh) karena**: neutral and can be used for any situation; can be placed either at the beginning or in the middle of the sentence
- **(Oleh) sebab**: neutral; cannot be placed at the beginning of the sentence
- **Gara-gara**: from Javanese **goro-goro**; means 'as a result of'; can occur either at the beginning or in the middle of the sentence
- **Lantaran**: for informal use; can be placed either at the beginning or in the middle of the sentence

22 Ways to Say 'If'

22.1 If

There are various ways to say 'if' in Indonesian, each differing in terms of formality and the likelihood of the event happening. These are called *conditionals*.

In this chapter we look at five common ways to say 'if'.

- **kalau**
- **jika**
- **(apa)bila**
- **seumpama(nya)**
- **seandainya**

Kalau

Kalau is the common and most neutral way of saying 'if'. That is, it is neither too formal nor informal, so we can use it for any situation. It can be placed at the beginning or in the middle of a sentence.

> **Kalau hujan, kita tidak akan pergi.**
> If it rains, we will not go.
>
> **Saya tidak mau ikut kalau kamu tidak menjemput saya.**
> I won't come along if you don't pick me up.
>
> **Jangan parkir mobil di situ kalau tidak mau didenda.**
> Don't park your car there if (you) don't want to be fined.

Jika and *(apa)bila*

Jika and **(apa)bila** are more formal or poetic than **kalau**. They mean the same thing, but you probably would not want to use them with friends. These words are more appropriate in writing, songs or public announcements. As with **kalau**, we can place **jika** and **(apa)bila** at the beginning or in the middle of a sentence. **Apabila** is often shortened into **bila**, which is why **apa** is shown in parentheses.

Jika ada rejeki, kami ingin mengunjungi Singapura.
If we had some good fortune, we would like to visit Singapore.

Kami akan naik haji tahun depan apa(bila) tidak ada aral melintang.
We will go on a pilgrimage to Mecca next year if everything goes well (literally: 'if there are no obstacles').

Jangan membuka email itu jika tidak mau komputer anda terserang virus.
Don't open that e-mail if (you) don't want your computer to be affected by the virus.

LATIHAN 1

KOSAKATA	
cuaca	weather
keras-keras	loudly
lapar	hungry
lulus ujian	to pass an exam
mogok	to break down

Complete the following sentences. Each sentence contains **kalau**, **jika** or **(apa)bila**. You may need to consult your dictionary for this exercise.

1 Jika cuaca baik, ...
2 Kalau mobil anda mogok, ...
3 Bila gigi anda sakit, ...
4 Jika tidak makan pagi, ...
5 Kalau saya punya uang, ...
6 Kalau lulus ujian, ...
7 Jika anda berbicara keras-keras, ...
8 Jika tidak boleh menonton televisi, ...
9 Apabila tidak boleh pergi, ...
10 Kalau kamu lapar, ...

Seumpama(nya)

Seumpama(nya) is used to say 'if' when we know that the likelihood of the event happening is not great. Like **kalau**, **jika** and **(apa)bila**, **seumpama** can be placed at the beginning or in the middle of a sentence. The suffix **-nya** is optional.

Seumpama dia datang, tolong beritahu saya.
If she comes, please let me know.
(I don't think she will come, but if she does, please tell me.)

Kamu akan bilang apa seumpama dia marah?
What will you say if he gets angry?
(I don't think he will get angry, but if he does, what will you say?)

Note
Sometimes people add two 'if' words together for emphasis. **Seumpama** combines well with **kalau**, since both are neutral in terms of formality.

Kalau seumpama(nya) ...

Seandainya

Seandainya is similar to **seumpama**, but it is more formal and is usually used when we want to say that there is little likelihood of the event happening. **Seandainya** can be placed at the beginning or in the middle of a sentence.

Seandainya saya milyuner, saya akan membeli kapal pesiar yang mewah.
If I were a millionaire, I would buy a luxury yacht.

Kami akan berpesta besar seandainya kami menang lotre.
We would have a big party if we won the lottery.

Note
As with **seumpama(nya)**, people often add **seandainya** with **jika** or **(apa)bila**. These words are compatible, since both are rather formal.

Jika seandainya ...
(Apa)bila seandainya ...

LATIHAN 2

The following are the lyrics of a popular song written by Indonesian songwriter and singer Melly Goeslaw. The song contains two of the 'if' words: **jika** and **seumpama**. Translate the song into English. Some of the vocabulary is given below; however, you may need your teacher's help in interpreting the song.

Jika
by Melly Goeslaw and Ari Lasso

Jika teringat tentang dikau
Jauh di mata dekat di hati
Sempat terpikir 'tuk kembali
Walau beda akan kujalani
Tak ada niat untuk selamanya pergi.

Jika teringat tentang dikau
Jauh di mata dekat di hati
Apakah sama yang kurasa
Ingin jumpa walau ada segan
Tak ada niat untuk berpisah denganmu.

Jika memang masih bisa mulutku berbicara
Santun kata yang ingin terucap
'Kan kudengar caci dan puji dirimu padaku
Kita masih muda dalam mencari keputusan
Maafkan daku ingin kembali
Seumpama ada jalan 'tuk kembali.

KOSAKATA

beda	different
berpisah	to part
caci	swearing
daku	I
dikau	you
dirimu	you
jumpa	to meet, see someone
'kan (from **akan**)	will
kembali	to return, get back together
keputusan	decision
kujalani	I will do it
kurasa	I feel
memang	indeed
mulut	mouth
niat	intention
puji	compliment
santun kata	the words
segan	reluctance
teringat	to remember
terpikir	to occur to me
terucap	uttered
'tuk (from **untuk**)	for, to

22.2 If ... then ...

- **kalau ... maka**
- **jika ... maka**
- **(apa)bila ... maka**
- **seumpama(nya) ... maka**
- **seandainya ... maka**

To say 'if ..., then ...', we simply add **maka** after the 'if' word.

Kalau/jika/(apa)bila kamu seperti itu, maka saya tidak mau pergi denganmu.
If you're like that, then I don't want to go with you.

Seumpama(nya)/seandainya hal itu terjadi, maka kami akan segera bertindak.
If that happened, then we would immediately take action.

Handy expression
To say 'if so' or 'if that's the case', we can say **kalau begitu** or, if we want to sound formal, **jika/(apa)bila demikian.**

Kalau begitu, saya pulang sekarang.
If so, I'm going home now.

Jika/(apa)bila demikian, kami pulang sekarang.
If that's the case, we're going home now.

To say 'if you don't mind':

Kalau (kamu/anda/Bapak/Ibu) tidak keberatan.

22.3 If only

- **kalau saja ...**
- **jika saja ...**
- **(apa)bila saja ...**
- **seumpama(nya) saja ...**
- **seandainya saja ...**

To say 'if only', we add **saja** to **kalau**, **jika**, **seumpama(nya)** and **seandainya**.

Kalau saja kamu datang sore itu!
If only you came that afternoon!

Jika/(apa)bila saja polisi cepat menangkap pencuri itu!
If only the police quickly captured that thief!

Seumpama(nya) saja dia tidak menabrak pohon itu.
If only he/she didn't hit that tree!

Seandainya saja gempa bumi itu tidak terjadi!
If only that earthquake didn't happen!

22.4 What if ...?

- **bagaimana kalau**
- **bagamana jika**
- **bagaimana (apa)bila**
- **bagaimana seumpama(nya)**
- **bagaimana seandainya**

To say 'What if ...?', we add **bagaimana** in front of the four 'if' words.

Bagaimana kalau hujan?
What if it rains?

Bagaimana jika/(apa)bila kami kalah?
What if we lose?

Bagaimana seumpama kamu dapat hadiah tiket ke Bali pulang-pergi?
What if you get a gift of a return ticket to Bali?

Bagaimana seandainya kamu melihat hantu itu?
What if you see that ghost?

LATIHAN 3

Say the following sentences in Indonesian. Choose the appropriate 'if' word for the situation and the person to whom you are talking.

1 Ask your friend: 'What if you're that teacher?'
2 Ask your teacher: 'Will we play basketball if it rains?'
3 Say to a stranger: 'What if I give you a million dollars?'
4 Heading for a magazine article: 'What if the world is not round?'
5 Say this to the class: 'What if we die tomorrow?'

Translate the following sentences into Indonesian. The Indonesian equivalents of the underlined words are given in parentheses.

6 If only they could lend us some money, we would not be this miserable. (**sengsara**)
7 What if she doesn't love you any more?
8 What if you could travel overseas tomorrow? (**pergi ke luar negeri**)
9 What if they don't want you to go with them?
10 If only I got a scholarship, I could study in Indonesia. (**beasiswa**)

Summary

- Five ways of saying 'if':
  —**Kalau**: neutral; can be used in any situation
  —**Jika/(apa)bila**: more formal or poetic; appropriate for writing or public announcements
  —**Seumpama(nya)**: neutral; less likelihood of event happening
  —**Seandainya**: formal; less likelihood of event happening
- If ... then: 'if' word ... + **maka**
- If only: 'if' word + **saja**
- What if ...?: **bagaimana** + 'if' word

23

When and While

This chapter looks at ways of saying 'when' and 'while' in Indonesian. These words are used to connect one part of a sentence to another.

In grammatical terms, these are called *conjunctions* and in Indonesian we can use the following words.

- **ketika**
- **waktu**
- **sementara**
- **sambil**
- **sedangkan**

23.1 *Ketika* and *waktu*

Ketika and **waktu** both mean 'when', but **ketika** is a little more formal than **waktu**. These words are used to point to something that either happened in the past or will happen.

Waktu/ketika saya kecil keluarga saya tinggal di Surabaya.
When I was little (a child) my family lived in Surabaya.

Kami sedang tidur waktu/ketika polisi datang ke rumah.
We were sleeping when the police came to our house.

Ruth akan menelepon waktu/ketika sampai di Brisbane.
Ruth will ring when she arrives in Brisbane.

Be careful!
To use 'when' as a question word (see Chapter 1), use **kapan**.

Kapan kamu pulang?
When are you going home?

Never use **kapan** as a conjunction, even though in English it also translates as 'when'. We cannot say, for instance:

- **Saya tinggal di Surabaya kapan saya kecil.**
  I lived in Surabaya when I was little (a child).

23.2 Sementara

Sementara means 'while' in the sense of 'someone does something, while someone else does something else' or 'something happens while something else also happens'.

Kakak perempuan saya memasak <u>sementara</u> ibu pergi berbelanja.
My older sister cooked <u>while</u> my mother went shopping.

Pada bulan Desember di Eropa turun salju, <u>sementara</u> di Australia cuaca panas.
In December, in Europe it snows, <u>while</u> in Australia it is hot.

Tuti tertawa <u>sementara</u> ketiga temannya menangis.

23.3 Sambil

In contrast to **sementara**, which is used either for different people doing different things at the same time or for different things happening at the same time, **sambil** is used to refer to the same person(s) or animal(s) doing two things at the same time. It can be placed either at the beginning or in the middle of a sentence.

Rio makan <u>sambil</u> menonton televisi.
Rio is eating <u>while</u> watching television.

<u>Sambil</u> meringkik kuda itu berlari.
<u>While</u> neighing the horse ran.

Handy expression
To say 'to kill two birds with one stone' (to do two things simultaneously) in Indonesian, we would say **sambil menyelam minum air**, which literally means 'while swimming underwater, drink the water'. This expression can also be used to mean 'to take advantage of something else at the same time of doing something'.

23.4 *Sedangkan*

Sedangkan means 'while' or 'whereas, where in fact'. We can use it to contrast two things, such as people, likes and dislikes or qualities.

Jalan Mawar lebar and bagus, sedangkan jalan Kenanga sempit dan kotor.
Mawar Street is wide and neat, while Kenanga Street is narrow and dirty.

Adik saya suka bersepeda, sedangkan kakak saya gemar bersepeda motor.
My younger sibling likes cycling, while my older one loves riding a motorbike.

LATIHAN 1

Join the two parts of each sentence using an appropriate 'when' or 'while' word. There may be more than one possible answer for each sentence. You may need to consult your dictionary for this exercise.

1 Kulit pisang warnanya kuning ________________ kulit buah kiwi warnanya coklat.
2 Ani berbicara ________________ menangis.
3 John naik bis ke kampus ________________ Linda bersepeda.
4 Lily berasal dari Cina ________________ Felix dari Nigeria
5 Anak kecil itu mandi ________________ bernyanyi.
6 Saya sedang mendengarkan walkman ________________ ibu saya pulang dari kantor.
7 Guru mengoreksi pekerjaan ________________ murid-murid murid-murid mengerjakan latihan tata bahasa.
8 Gaji pegawai tidak naik ________________ harga bahan pangan terus meningkat.
9 Burung-burung beterbangan ________________ berkicau.
10 Kami ke sekolah ________________ ibu pergi bekerja.

LATIHAN 2

Look at the following picture of a busy street. Describe what people are doing using **sambil**, **sementara** or **sedangkan**. You may need to consult your dictionary for this exercise.

Example:

Nenek ini sedang berjalan, sedangkan anak kecil itu bermain di kolam.

This grandmother is walking, while the small child is playing in the pond.

Summary

Ways of saying 'when' and 'while':

- **Ketika** and **waktu**; for something which takes place in the past or future
- **Sementara**; for when two different persons are doing different things at the same time, or when two different things happen at the same time
- **Sambil**; for when someone does two things at the same time
- **Sedangkan**; for contrasting two things

24

Although and Not … But

In this chapter we will learn how to say:
- 'although', 'even though', 'even if', 'although it is so', 'in spite of'
- 'not … but', 'not only … but also', 'rather than … in fact', 'not only … on the contrary'

24.1 Although, even though

To say 'although' and 'even though' in Indonesian, we can choose between the following words.

- **meski(pun)**
- **walau(pun)**
- **biar(pun)**

The ending **pun** in those three words is shown in parentheses because people often omit it when they speak or write. The omission of **pun** can also make the words sound more poetic, which is why people tend to omit it when writing songs or poetry.

We can place these words either at the beginning or in the middle of a sentence.

> **Meski(pun) hujan, Rani datang juga ke rumah saya.**
> Even though it rained, Rani still came to my house.
>
> **Dia tetap saja tidak mau belajar walau(pun) tahu ujian sudah dekat.**
> He/she still doesn't want to study, although (he/she) knows the exam is near.
>
> **Biar(pun) sudah dua kali dipenjara, orang itu masih merampok juga.**
> Even though twice jailed, that person still robs.

Even if

Meski(pun), **walau(pun)** and **biar(pun)** can also mean 'even if', depending on what we intend to say.

> **Meski(pun) hujan, kita masih bisa pergi.**
> Even if it rains, we can still go.

Tanaman itu akan tetap tumbuh walau(pun) tidak disiram.
That plant will still grow even if you don't water it.

Mereka tetap akan membuang sampah di situ biar(pun) lubang itu ditutup.
They will still throw rubbish there even if the hole is covered.

Although it is so, in spite of

- **meski(pun) begitu**
- **meski(pun) demikian**
- **walau(pun) begitu**
- **walau(pun) demikian**
- **biar(pun) begitu**
- **biar(pun) demikian**

Meski(pun), **walau(pun)** and **biar(pun)** are often combined with either **begitu** or **demikian** to mean 'in spite of that' or 'although/even though it is so'. **Demikian** is more formal, so it is not suitable to use when talking to close friends.

Meski(pun) begitu/demikian, saya tetap baik kepadanya.
In spite of that, I still treat him/her well.

Walau(pun) begitu/demikian, kami tetap percaya kepada mereka.
In spite of that, we still trust them.

Biar(pun) begitu/demikian, mereka masih saja tidak bisa menerima saran kami.
In spite of that, they still cannot accept our suggestion.

Note
One of the meanings of **begitu** and **demikian** is 'so'. However, because neither of these words can stand alone, we cannot use them to say, for example, 'He didn't come, so I went home'. **Begitu** and **demikian** only mean 'so' in the sense of 'even though/although it is so' (as in the above examples) or 'it is so ... that ...' ('to the extent that').

Film itu begitu/demikian panjangnya sehingga saya jadi bosan.
The film was so long that I got bored.

LATIHAN 1

Translate the following sentences with **meski(pun)**, **walau(pun)** and **biar(pun)** into English. You may need to consult your dictionary for this exercise.

1. Meskipun harga tiket pesawat terbang mahal, kami pergi juga ke Bali.
2. Walaupun demikian, dia tidak mau minta tolong pada saya.
3. Biarpun acara televisi jelek, saya menonton juga.

4 Meski cuaca dingin, Joni tidak memakai jaket.
5 Walau guru marah, murid-murid tidak berhenti bercakap-cakap.
6 Biar sering disiram, pohon itu tidak cepat tumbuh.
7 Biarpun dibayar 10 juta rupiah, saya tidak mau membantu orang seperti dia.
8 Guru itu baik walaupun tidak banyak tersenyum.
9 Jeremy pergi ke pertandingan sepak bola itu meskipun harga karcisnya mahal.
10 Dia terus mengirim email kepada saya meskipun saya tidak pernah membalasnya.

24.2 Not ... but

- **bukan ... tetapi**
- **bukan ... namun**
- **bukan ... melainkan**

There are different ways of saying 'not ... but ...' in Indonesian. The first three expressions in the box above differ in terms of formality. **Bukan ... tetapi** is the most neutral, so we can use it for any situation, spoken or written. **Bukan ... namun** and **bukan ... melainkan** mean the same thing, but are more formal. They are therefore more suitable for use in formal speech (for example, with someone older or unfamiliar to you) or in writing. The difference between these expressions is similar to the difference between 'but' and 'however' in English.

Bukan ini, tetapi itu.
Not this, but that.

Bukan kami enggan, namun kami memang benar-benar tidak bisa membantu.
It's not that we're reluctant, but we in fact really couldn't help.

Bukan kesehatan bapak saya yang merisaukan, melainkan kesehatan ibu.
It's not my father's health that is worrying, but my mother's.

Not only ... but also

- **bukan saja ... tetapi juga**
- **bukan saja ... namun juga**

To say 'not only ... but also', we simply add **saja** after **bukan**, and **juga** after **tetapi** or **namun**.

Bukan saja dia malas, tetapi juga sering berbohong.
Not only is he/she lazy, but (he/she) also often lies.

Bukan saja dia pandai, namun juga baik hati.
Not only is he/she smart, but (he/she) is also good-hearted.

LATIHAN 2

Say the following in Indonesian, using the expressions that you have learnt.
Choose between **tetapi**, **namun** and **melainkan** for 'but' and specify to whom you are talking or on what occasion.

1 The party is not at my house, but in their house.
2 The exam is not only long, but also very difficult.
3 The merchandise in that shop is not only expensive, but also of low quality.
4 This city is not only large, but also beautiful.
5 We are not only happy you came, but also grateful.

KOSAKATA

barang merchandise
berkualitas rendah of low quality
berterima kasih grateful

Rather than ... in fact

- **bukannya ... malahan ...**

Another expression related to the ones above is **bukannya ... malahan ...** (rather than ... in fact ...). The table below shows how we can structure our sentence when using this expression.

BUKANNYA	VERB	SUBJECT	MALAHAN	VERB
Bukannya	**diam**	**tangisnya**	**malahan**	**menjadi-jadi.**
Rather than	stopping (being quiet)	his/her cry	in fact	became worse.
Bukannya	**membantu**	**dia**	**malahan**	**berdiri saja menonton.**
Rather than	helping	he/she	in fact	just stood there watching.

Not ... on the contrary

- **bukannya ... tetapi malahan ...**

We can also add **tetapi** or **namun** before **malahan** to mean 'not ... on the contrary' or 'instead of ... he/she just ...'. To use it in a sentence, we can put the words in the following order.

SUBJECT	BUKANNYA	VERB	TETAPI MALAHAN	VERB
Hartono	**bukannya**	**menjawab ketika dipanggil**	**tetapi malahan**	**ngeloyor pergi.**
Hartono	did not	answer when called;	on the contrary,	(he/she) just left.
(Instead of answering when called, he/she just left.)				
Mereka	**bukannya**	**mendengar -kan**	**tetapi malahan**	**menertawa-kan kami.**
They	did not	listen (to us);	on the contrary,	they laughed at us.
(Instead of listening (to us), they just laughed at us.)				

LATIHAN 3

Complete the following sentences, then translate them into English. You may need to consult your dictionary for this exercise.

1 Bukannya tidur dia malahan ______________________
2 Bukannya ______________________ Andreas malahan membaca majalah.
3 Bukannya makan nasi ______________________ malahan ______________________
4 Bukannya minta maaf ______________________ malahan ______________________
5 Bukannya ______________________ malahan meminjam uang kepada saya.
6 ______________________ bukannya ______________________ tetapi malahan tidur sampai siang.
7 Paman saya bukannya ______________________ tetapi malahan ______________________
8 ______________________ bukannya ______________________ tetapi malahan menabrak mobil merah itu.
9 Burung itu bukannya ______________________ tetapi malahan ______________________
10 ______________________ bukannya takut tetapi malahan ______________________

Summary

To say:

- 'although', 'even though', 'even if':
  —**meski(pun), walau(pun), biar(pun)**
- 'although it is so', 'in spite of':
  —**meski(pun)/walau(pun)/biar(pun) begitu**
  —**meski(pun)/walau(pun)/biar(pun) demikian**
- 'not … but': **bukan … tetapi/namun/melainkan**
- 'not only … but also': **bukan … tetapi/namun/melainkan juga**
- 'rather than … in fact': **bukannya … malahan**
- 'not only … on the contrary': **bukannya … tetapi malahan**

25

The ... More ... the ... More ...

The expression 'the more ... the more ...' indicates that something or someone undergoes a gradual change in condition or proportion.

In Indonesian we can use the following expressions to indicate such a change.

- **makin ... makin ...**
- **(ber)tambah ... (ber)tambah ...**
- **kian ... kian ...**

25.1 *Makin ... makin ...*

Makin is neutral in terms of formality, so we can use it for any situation.

Rita	**makin lama**	**makin sombong.**
Rita	the longer	the more arrogant.

→ Rita is getting more and more arrogant.

Harga bensin	**makin hari**	**makin naik.**
The price of petrol	by the day	increases more.

→ The price of petrol goes up every day.

We can also put the noun or noun phrase, such as 'Rita' or **harga bensin**, after the first **makin** phrase.

Makin lama Rita makin sombong.

Makin hari harga bensin makin naik.

Handy expression
To say 'the more the merrier' in Indonesian, we can use **makin banyak makin ramai**.

25.2 *(Ber)tambah ... (ber)tambah ...*

The expression **(ber)tambah ... (ber)tambah ...** means the same as **makin** and is used in the same way. The difference is, if we add the prefix **ber-** to **tambah**, it is a little more formal. As with **makin**, the noun (or noun phrase) can be placed at the beginning of the sentence or after the first **(ber)tambah** phrase.

Anak itu	**bertambah besar**	**bertambah cantik**	**parasnya.**
That child	the older	the more beautiful	her face.

→ That child is more beautiful the older she gets.

If we drop the prefix, the expression becomes less formal, like **makin**.

25.3 *Kian ... kian*

The expression **Kian ... kian** is more formal. The noun (or noun phrase) can be placed at the beginning of the sentence or after the first **kian** phrase.

Kami	**kian/hari**	**kian**	**jengkel.**
We	by the day	the more	annoyed.

→ We are getting more and more annoyed by the day.

LATIHAN 1

Copy and complete the following sentences, filling in the empty spaces.

KOSAKATA

cepat marah	quick to anger
kurus	thin, skinny
perusahaan	company
petani	farmer
sulit	difficult

NOUN (NOUN PHRASE)	*MAKIN, (BER)TAMBAH, KIAN*	*MAKIN, (BER)TAMBAH, KIAN*
1	makin lama	
2		makin kurus
3 Pemuda itu		
4	kian sukses	
5 Petani itu		

MAKIN, (BER)TAMBAH, KIAN	NOUN (NOUN PHRASE)	*MAKIN, (BER)TAMBAH, KIAN*
6	perokok itu	
7		makin sulit
8 Kian hari		
9		tambah cepat marah
10	direktur perusahaan itu	

Summary

- **Makin ... makin, (ber)tambah ... (ber)tambah** and **kian ... kian** all express a gradual change in condition or proportion.
- **Makin ... makin** and **tambah ... tambah** can be used for any situation, while **bertambah ... bertambah** and **kian ... kian** are more formal.
- To use them in a sentence: the noun (or noun phrase) can be placed either at the beginning or after the first **makin**, **(ber)tambah** or **kian** phrase.

26

Both ... and ... / ... As Well As ...

In Indonesian, the expression **baik ... maupun** is used to mean 'both ... and ...' or '... as well as ...'.

26.1 Baik ... maupun

Here are some examples of the use of **baik ... maupun**.

> **Baik ibu maupun bapak saya tidak makan daging.**
> Both my mother and father do not eat meat.
>
> **Demonstrasi itu berlangsung baik di kota besar maupun kota kecil.**
> The demonstration took place both in big cities and small towns.
>
> **Anda bisa ke sana baik naik pesawat terbang maupun kapal laut.**
> You can go there both by plane and by boat.

LATIHAN 1

Write five sentences using **baik ... maupun**.

Example:

BAIK + SOMEONE	*MAUPUN* + SOMEONE ELSE	DO OR DON'T DO SOMETHING
Baik Rudi Both Rudi	**maupun Ani** and Ani	**tidak masuk sekolah hari ini.** did not go to school today.

Write five more sentences using **baik ... maupun** in a different way.

Example:

SOMETHING HAPPENS	*BAIK* + SOMEWHERE	*MAUPUN* + SOMEWHERE ELSE
Terjadi gempa bumi There was an earthquake	**baik di Jawa** both in Java	**maupun di Bali.** and in Bali.

LATIHAN 2

Translate these sentences into English. You may need to consult your dictionary for this exercise.

1 Baik kakak maupun adik saya suka musik dangdut.
2 Hotel itu memiliki bermacam-macam fasilitas, baik untuk rekreasi maupun bisnis.
3 Baik mie goreng maupun nasi goreng harganya sama.
4 Siapapun dilarang masuk pabrik itu, baik pegawai maupun bukan pegawai.
5 Baik kopi maupun teh mengandung kafein.
6 Penerbit Gramedia di Jakarta menerbitkan bermacam-macam buku, baik buku cerita anak-anak maupun buku ilmiah.
7 Robert selalu memakai celana pendek, baik pada musim panas maupun musim dingin.
8 Baik pisang maupun pepaya banyak mengandung vitamin.
9 Sopir taksi itu bekerja keras baik siang maupun malam.
10 Baik berjalan kaki maupun berenang adalah baik untuk kesehatan.

Summary

Baik … maupun translates into English as 'both … and …' or '… as well as …'. It is used to refer to two things, two people, two places or two actions of comparable qualities or conditions.

21

Let Alone

To say 'let alone ..., even ...' in Indonesian, we have the following choices.

- **jangankan ... , ... pun/saja ...**
- **apalagi ... , ... saja ...**
- **kok ..., ... saja ...**
- **boro-boro ..., ... saja ...**

The last two of these expressions are more informal than the others and are used more in speaking than in writing.

21.1 *Jangankan ... pun/saja*

Jangankan (let alone) is usually placed at the beginning of a sentence, while **pun** or **saja** comes in the second part of the sentence.

> **Jangankan ke Australia, ke Jakarta pun saya tidak mampu.**
> Let alone go to Australia; I can't even afford to go to Jakarta.
>
> **Jangankan berpidato, berbicara saja dia tidak becus.**
> Let alone make a speech; he/she can't even speak properly.

21.2 *Apalagi ... saja*

Apalagi can be placed either at the beginning or in the middle of a sentence.

> **Apalagi kamu, saya saja tidak boleh masuk.**
> Let alone you, even I'm not allowed to go in.
>
> **Saya saja tidak boleh masuk, apalagi kamu.**
> Even I'm not allowed to go in, let alone you.

LATIHAN 1

Write five sentences using **jangankan ... pun/saja**.

Example:

JANGANKAN + DO SOMETHING	DO SOMETHING ELSE + *PUN* OR *SAJA*	SUBJECT DOESN'T/CAN'T DO
Jangankan makan buah, Let alone eat fruit,	**makan nasi pun** even eating rice	**dia tidak mau.** he/she doesn't want to do.

Write five sentences using **apalagi**.

Example:

SUBJECT + *SAJA*	CANNOT DO SOMETHING	*APALAGI* + SOMEBODY ELSE
Dia saja Even he/she	**tidak bisa memecahkan persoalan itu** cannot solve the problem,	**apalagi kamu.** let alone you.

27.3 *Kok ... saja* and *boro-boro ... saja*

As mentioned at the beginning of the chapter, sentences with **kok ... saja** and **boro-boro ... saja** are informal and therefore are usually for informal spoken situations.

> **Kok beli mobil, untuk makan saja gaji saya tidak cukup.**
> Let alone buy a car, even to buy food my salary is not enough.
>
> **Boro-boro menang undian, beli karcisnya saja dia tidak pernah.**
> Let alone win a raffle, he/she never even buys tickets.

LATIHAN 2

Write five sentences using **kok ... saja**.

Example:

KOK + SOMEONE	SOMEBODY ELSE + *SAJA*	DOESN'T/CAN'T DO SOMETHING
Kok perawat itu, Let alone that nurse,	**dokter saja** even the doctor	**tidak bisa menyembuhkan dia.** cannot cure him/her

Write five sentences using **boro-boro ... saja**.

Example:

BORO-BORO + DO SOMETHING	DO SOMETHING ELSE + *SAJA*	SUBJECT DOESN'T/ CAN'T DO
Boro-boro ke sekolah, Let alone go to school,	**bangun saja** even getting up	**saya tidak bisa.** I cannot do.

Summary

- **Jangankan, apalagi, kok and boro-boro** all mean 'let alone'; they are paired with either **pun** or **saja** (even).
- **Pun** is more formal and is therefore compatible with **jangankan**.
- **Jangankan** is placed at the beginning of the sentence.
- **Apalagi** can appear either at the beginning or in the middle of the sentence.
- **Kok** and **boro-boro** are more informal and are appropriate for casual conversation.

28

Imperatives

Imperatives are the language forms that we use to tell people to do things. This may mean giving commands, making requests, offering, inviting, urging or advising. We also use imperatives to tell people not to do something (prohibiting). These imperatives are called *negative imperatives.*

The forms that we use often depend on such things as when, where and to whom we are talking or writing. For example, the form that a teacher uses to give a command to his or her students in a classroom situation would generally be different from that used by two close friends. The first would be more formal, while the second would be less formal.

Also, certain forms tend to be used only in writing, while others are more commonly used in speaking.

In this chapter we look at these different forms and learn:

- how to choose which form(s) to use and for whom
- for which communicative situations they are appropriate

28.1 Commands

Commands are instructions to tell people to do something, often immediately. In English, we might say 'Stand up!', 'Go to bed!', 'Eat your dinner!' and so forth. In Indonesian, the common forms to use vary, depending on whether the verb is transitive or intransitive. If the verb is transitive, the forms to use vary, depending on whether the object is specific or non-specific.

Commands using intransitive verbs

In intransitive sentences, the form of the verb does not change. So, if the verb has the prefix **ber-**, this prefix remains. For example, a teacher may say this to his or her students:

> **Berdiri!**
> Stand up!

Similarly, if the verb has the prefix **meN-**, we keep this prefix. For example, if the same teacher wants the students to simply write, without specifying what to write, he or she will say:

> **Menulis.**
> Write.

The prefix is still retained even if the teacher specifies when the action is to be performed (for example, 'now' or 'later'), because there is no object involved.

> **Membaca dahulu lalu istirahat.**
> Read first, then rest.

For simple verbs, such as **makan**, that do not require an affix, nothing is added. Thus a mother may say to her ten-year-old daughter, who is a reluctant eater:

> **Makan**!
> Eat!

Commands using transitive verbs

In transitive sentences, the prefix **meN-** is dropped if the object is specific. For example, if your teacher tells you to write not simply any letter, but a letter to your penfriend, he or she will say:

> **Tulis surat kepada sahabat penamu.**
> Write a letter to your penfriend.

Not:

> **Menulis surat kepada sahabat penamu.**

Similarly, **meN-** is dropped in the following sentences.

> **Buka halaman 5.**
> Open page 5.

> **Buka pintu itu!**
> Open the door!

Did you know?
Tone of voice has a lot to do with how our commands are interpreted. Commands may sound harsh or may be considered impolite if they are expressed in a strong or abrupt tone of voice. A softer tone may give an impression that the commands are polite and friendly.

How to make commands more informal

- **ayo**
- **coba**
- **ya**
- **dong**

The imperative forms that we use often depend on when, where and to whom we are talking or writing. Formal situations require more formal forms, whereas informal situations are suitable for less formal forms. Different imperative forms express different degrees of formality. The more formal a form, the more polite it is generally considered to be. However, this does not mean that informal forms are always impolite. They can be so only if we misjudge the relation that we have as a speaker with the person(s) to whom we are speaking. We can inadvertently offend people by using inappropriate forms.

To make commands less formal, we can add **ayo**, **coba**, **ya** or **dong**.

AYO AND *COBA*

The teacher giving the commands that we looked at on pages 167–8 could say the following instead.

Ayo, berdiri!
Come on, stand up!

Ayo, menulis!
Come on, write!

Ayo, tulis surat kepada sahabat penamu!
Come on, write a letter to your penfriend!

Coba, buka halaman 5!
Come on, open page 5!

Coba, membaca dulu baru istirahat!
Come on, read first, then rest!

Coba, buka pintu itu!
Come on, open that door!

Similarly, the mother telling her daughter to eat could say instead:

Ayo, makan.
Come on, eat.

YA

Ya literally means 'yes'. When used in commands, it is similar to the 'won't you/will you' tag that is used in English. It is usually placed at the end of the sentence.

Tidur ya.
Go to sleep, won't you?

Makan ya.
Eat, won't you?

Note

Because **ya** can make a command quite soft, it is less suitable for situations that demand formality. The above commands, given by a mother to her child, certainly do not mean 'Do what I say right now', but rather something like 'It would be good if you did this now'.

In transitive sentences, **ya** can be placed either after the verb, to emphasise the action, or at the end, which then puts the focus on the whole command.

Lipat ya baju ini.
Lipat baju ini ya.
Fold this shirt, won't you?

Makan ya obatnya.
Makan obatnya ya.
Take the medication, won't you?

DONG

Dong is more informal than **ayo** and **ya** and, when used in commands, also roughly translates into English as 'won't you' or 'will you'. Like **ya**, **dong** can be placed either after the verb, to emphasise the action, or at the end of the command, to emphasise the whole command.

Be careful!

Because **dong** is informal, it is not an expression that we would use in situations that require us to observe formality, such as in ceremonial situations, public announcements or when speaking to strangers in the street or to guests. For example, one would not normally say to a priest: **Berkati saya dong** ('Please bless me') or to the guests at a formal function: **Duduk dong** ('Please sit down').

Dong is most appropriate when used among close friends and family members.

Berdiri dong.
Stand up, wont' you?

Pakai dong sepatumu.
Pakai sepatumu dong.
Wear your shoes, won't you?

Cuci mobilnya dong.
Cuci dong mobilnya.
Wash the car, won't you?

LATIHAN 1

Read the following commands and decide whether they are correct (**Benar**) or incorrect (**Salah**). Remember that the **meN-** prefix is dropped in transitive sentences if the object is specific.

1 Tidur di sana ya!
2 Coba menelepon temanmu itu!
3 Melihat foto saya!
4 Ayo, mendengarkan musik ini ya.
5 Coba, berlari ke sana!
6 Membawa anjingmu ke rumah saya ya.
7 Ayo mengetik artikel penting ini di komputer.
8 Makan buah dan sayur setiap hari ya.
9 Belikan saya es krim dong!
10 Menyimpan fotomu itu baik-baik!

KOSAKATA

membawa	to take
mengetik	to type
menyimpan	to keep, store
penting	important

How to make commands more formal

- **-lah**
- **harap**
- **hendaklah/hendaknya**
- **mohon**

We can make commands more polite and formal by adding different words or part words, such as **-lah**, **harap**, **hendaklah** or **hendaknya** and **mohon**. When we add these words, our commands also become more impersonal. Because of that, they would not be suitable for use with friends, family members or people with whom we have an informal relation.

-LAH

The suffix **-lah** is a *particle*. It is not commonly used in spoken Indonesian, but is included here because you are likely to come across it in short stories or novels. It is 'formal' in the sense that we would not use it in casual conversation. The addition of **-lah** in written Indonesian makes a command softer and it may be attached to both intransitive and transitive verbs.

Berdiri<u>lah</u>.
<u>Please</u> stand up.

Tulis<u>lah</u> surat kepada nenekmu.
<u>Please</u> write a letter to your grandmother.

Buka<u>lah</u> pintu itu.
<u>Please</u> open that door.

HARAP

Literally meaning 'to hope' or 'to expect', **harap** forms the intransitive verb **berharap** and the transitive verbs **mengharap** and **mengharapkan**. Its use in imperatives means something like 'you are expected to do this', even though it is usually translated into English as 'please'. It is appropriate for use in formal announcements, where the addressee is a group of people rather than an individual.

Harap is usually placed at the beginning of the command, if the addressee is not mentioned. When the addressee is mentioned, **harap** is usually placed after it.

<u>Harap</u> berdiri.
<u>Please</u> stand up.

Penumpang <u>harap</u> tetap duduk.
Passengers <u>please</u> remain seated.

MOHON

Mohon, which also translates as 'please' in English, is similar to **harap** in its formality. However, unlike **harap**, **mohon** has a sense of urgency and pleading. Like **harap**, **mohon** can be placed at the beginning of the sentence, to produce a more direct command, or after the mention of the addressee, to make the command a little more indirect.

<u>Mohon</u> balas surat ini segera.
<u>Please</u> reply to this letter immediately.

Kami <u>mohon</u> hadirin tetap tenang
Literally: We ask you (the audience) to remain calm. → <u>Please</u> remain calm.

Saya <u>mohon</u> anda pergi dari sini.
Literally: I ask you to leave → <u>Please</u> get out of here.

HENDAKLAH AND *HENDAKNYA*

The word **hendak** forms a part of the noun **kehendak**, meaning 'a will or wish (to do something)'. By itself, without the prefix, it is used to indicate future action; for example, **Mereka hendak datang ke rumah saya** (They are going to come to my house). When used in commands, either **-lah** or **-nya** is attached to it. Because of their very formal nature, **hendaklah** and **hendaknya** are not common in everyday spoken Indonesian and are suitable for telling people to do abstract actions.

<u>Hendaklah</u> hal ini menjadi perhatian kita semua.
<u>Let this</u> matter become our concern.

Hendaklah/hendaknya can also be used for reprimanding very formally.

> **Hendaknya Saudara mengerti betul hal ini.**
> **Saudara hendaknya mengerti betul hal ini.**
> You should really understand this.

LATIHAN 2

You will find a wealth of imperatives in recipes. Below is a recipe for a Thai dessert from *Femina*, an Indonesian women's magazine. Translate the recipe into English. You may need to consult your dictionary for this exercise.

Ketan saus mangga

Bahan:

200 g	beras ketan putih
100 mL	santan kental
3 sdm	gula pasir
1/2 sdt	garam
1 lembar	daun pandan
2 buah (350 g)	mangga masak pohon, kupas, iris tipis daging buahnya

Saus:

100 mL	santan kental, rebus
1 sdm	gula pasir halus
1/4 sdt	garam

Cara membuat:

- Cuci beras ketan, tiriskan. Kukus beras ketan dalam dandang sampai ketan setengah matang. Angkat.
- Aduk ketan kukus bersama santan, gula pasir, dan garam hingga santan terhisap oleh ketan.
- Kukus kembali ketan dan daun pandan dalam dandang panas sampai matang. Angkat.
- Saus: Aduk santan kental dan gula hingga gula larut.
- Hidangkan ketan kukus bersama sausnya dan irisan mangga.

Untuk 6 orang
Kalori per porsi: 275
sdm = sendok makan
sdt = sendok teh

Femina no. 14/XXV, 10–16 April 1997, p. 177

Did you know?

Gula pasir literally means 'sand sugar', because the granules look like sand. 'Icing sugar' is **gula halus**, which literally means fine or smooth sugar (because it is in powder form).

Beras ketan means 'glutinous rice'. Have you seen or tasted it? If not, next time you go to an Asian grocery, you might like to buy some.

Did you know these different words for 'rice' in Indonesian?

padi	rice plant
beras	uncooked rice
beras merah	red rice (in Indonesia, often given as a food supplement for babies)
nasi	cooked rice
nasi putih	plain steamed rice
nasi goreng	fried rice
ketan hitam	black glutinous rice (used for black rice pudding)

28.2 Requests

- **minta**

Requesting means that we are asking for something or to be allowed to do something. This is rather different from commands, where we are telling people to do something. Some examples of requests are:

- a boss requesting a document to be typed
- a student requesting an extension for an assignment
- a doctor requesting a blood test to be done on his or her patient
- a friend requesting help with homework

In Indonesian, the word **minta** can be used to ask for something. This use of **minta** in imperatives translates into English as 'Can I/we ...?'. Of course, requests are not restricted to this word; other verbs can be used as well, as we can see below.

Minta nasinya.
Can I have some rice?

Minta kertas dua lembar lagi.
Can I have two more sheets of paper?

Bagi kuenya.
Can I have a share of the cake?

Ketikkan surat ini.
Type this letter for me.

How to make requests more informal

- **ya**
- **dong**

As with commands, we can use **ya** and **dong** in certain situations to make our requests more informal and less abrupt.

Minta nasinya ya.
Minta nasinya dong.
Can I have some rice, please?

Bagi kuenya ya.
Bagi kuenya dong.
Share the cake, please.

Ketikkan surat ini ya.
Ketikkan surat ini dong.
Type this letter for me, please.

How to make requests more polite

- **tolong**
- **minta tolong**

Requests can be made more polite by adding the word **tolong**, which literally means 'help', but which, when used in requests, means 'please (do something)'. Because **tolong** is polite, but not overly formal, it can be used for a wide variety of situations and with different addressees (with friends, strangers, teachers, parents and so on). We should note that, even though **tolong** can be translated as 'please' in English, it cannot be used for offering (for example, 'Please eat', 'Please let me do it') or for invitations (for example, 'Please come to the party').

When we use **tolong**, the **meN-** prefix is dropped.

Tolong bantu saya.
Please help me.

Tolong pegangkan payung ini.
Please hold this umbrella (for me).

Tolong panggilkan polisi.
Please call the police (for me).

Tolong can be combined with **minta**, to make the request more urgent.

Minta tolong panggilkan polisi.
Please help call the police.

We can also combine **tolong** with **ya** and **dong**, to make polite but informal (and friendly) requests. **Ya** and **dong** can be placed either after **tolong**, to emphasise politeness, or at the end of the sentence, to emphasise the whole request.

Tolong ya jagakan tas saya.
Tolong jagakan tas saya ya.
Would you please mind my bag for me?

Tolong ya temani bapak ke toko.
Tolong temani bapak ke toko ya.
Would you please accompany father to the shop?

Very formal requests

- **sudilah (kiranya)**

If we want to make very formal and very polite requests to someone in a very high position, we can use **sudilah** or **sudilah kiranya**. These expressions mean 'I/we hope you are willing do this'. **Sudilah (kiranya)** is hardly used in spoken Indonesian because of its highly formal nature, so we certainly would not want to use it with friends or family.

> **Sudilah (kiranya) bapak Presiden menghadiri pertemuan kami.**
> We hope you, Mr President, are willing to attend our meeting.

LATIHAN 3

Use appropriate words for requesting in the following situations. Consider who you are talking to and choose the most suitable form for each request. The verb that you need to use is given in parentheses. (Drop the **meN-** prefix, if appropriate.)

1. You have an early appointment with the dentist tomorrow and you are not good at waking up early. Ask your brother to wake you up at 7 a.m. (**membangunkan**)
2. You have just rung your teacher at school to tell her that you are sick, but she was in class. Leave a message with the secretary to pass on to your teacher when she returns, informing her that you are sick. (**memberitahukan**)
3. You are about to send a payment for your annual magazine subscription through the mail. You want the magazine to send you a receipt. Write your request. **(mengirimkan)**

28.3 Inviting

- **mari**
- **ayo**
- **yuk**

Inviting can mean two things: we may invite someone to join in an activity, such as going to the movies, or we may invite someone to come to our place or to a function, such as a birthday party. Indonesian has different verbs to express these two meanings of inviting: **mengajak** and **mengundang**.

Inviting can be expressed as a question (for example, 'Would you like to go to the movies?') or as an imperative (for example, 'Let's go to the movies', 'Drop by any time'). In this chapter, we look at the imperative forms only.

We can use **mari** and **ayo** for inviting someone to join in an activity (**mengajak**). Both are usually placed at the beginning of a sentence and are very common in spoken Indonesian. The difference between them is in their degree of formality: **mari** is more formal than **ayo**.

Mari kita pulang.
Let's go home.

Ayo kita makan dulu.
Let's eat first.

Ayo jalan-jalan sore ini.
Let's go out this evening.

Ayo is often shortened to **yuk** and can be placed either at the beginning of the sentence or right at the end. **Yuk** is even less formal than **ayo** and, because of that, we can use it with friends. For instance, you can say the following to your close friend, but not to your teacher:

Yuk kita ke perpustakaan.
Kita ke perpustakaan yuk.
Let's go to the library.

We can also use **mari**, **ayo** and **yuk** to invite someone to our place or function (**mengundang**).

Mari mampir ke rumah.
Ayo mampir ke rumah.
Mampir ke rumah yuk.
Do drop by.

If we want to be polite and more formal, we can use **silakan** ('please') for **mengundang** (but not for **mengajak**). For example, you could say the following to your mother's friend who comes to visit.

Silakan masuk, Bu.
Please come in.

Silakan duduk, saya akan panggil ibu saya.
Please sit down; I will call my mother.

With your friends, however, you may prefer to use **ya** or **dong** alongside the verb. Your offers would resemble commands when you do this.

Masuk dong, jangan di luar.
Come in; don't stay outside.

Duduk dulu ya, saya ke kamar sebentar.
Have a seat; I have to go to my room for a minute.

Datang ya ke pesta saya.
Datang dong ke pesta saya.
Come to my party.

LATIHAN 4

Use appropriate words for inviting in the following situations. Consider who you are talking to and choose the most suitable form for each invitation. The verbs are given in parentheses. (Drop the **meN-** prefix, if appropriate.)

1 Invite your close friend to come and <u>stay the night</u> at your place. (**menginap**)
2 Invite your younger sister to go and <u>have a coffee</u> with you. (**minum kopi**)
3 Invite your friend's parents to <u>come</u> to your school concert on Saturday. (**datang**)

28.4 Offering

- **ayo**
- **mari**
- **biar**

Offering can be understood to mean 'offering to do something for someone' or 'offering something to someone'. We can express the first meaning using **ayo**, **mari** and **biar**—all of which roughly mean '(come on, here) let me (or someone else) do it' when used in offering. All of them are placed at the beginning of the sentence.

As with the other uses, **ayo** makes the imperative more informal. However, its use here differs from the previous ones in that here the action is to be performed by the speaker, not the addressee. As in invitation, **mari** is more polite and formal. **Biar**, on the other hand, is polite, but neutral in terms of formality.

<u>Ayo</u> saya cucikan bajunya.
<u>Come on</u>, let me wash the clothes for you.

<u>Mari</u> saya bawakan kopernya.
<u>Here</u>, let me carry the suitcase for you.

<u>Biar</u> bapak saya yang mengantarkan dia ke sekolah.
<u>Let</u> my father take her to school.

The second sense of offering is expressed by using **silakan** and also **ayo**. As with their use in invitation, the difference between these two words lies in their degree of formality: **silakan** is more formal than **ayo**.

<u>Silakan</u> minum.
<u>Ayo</u> minum.
<u>Please</u> drink.

LATIHAN 5

Use appropriate words for offering in the following situations. Consider who you are talking to and choose the most suitable form for each offer. The verbs are given in parentheses. (Drop the **meN-** prefix, if appropriate.)

1 Your older sister has just said that she will make a cup of coffee. Offer to <u>make</u> one for her. (**membuatkan**)

2 Your mother is going to put your little brother to bed. Offer to do that for her. (**menidurkan**)
3 You have an exciting job promoting Australian apples in Indonesia. Encourage passers-by to try the apples. (**mencoba**)

28.5 Advising

- **sebaiknya**

A word that we can use to give advice to people is **sebaiknya**, meaning 'it is best that' or 'you had better'. This word is polite and a little formal.

> **Sebaiknya kau tanya ibumu dulu.**
> **Kau sebaiknya tanya ibumu dulu.**
> It is best that you ask your mother first/You had better ask your mother first.

Although **sebaiknya** is generally used for advising, it can also be used to give a polite command and can be placed either at the beginning of the sentence or after the mention of the addressee.

> **Sebaiknya Saudara keluar kelas.**
> **Saudara sebaiknya keluar kelas.**
> It is best that you leave this class/You had better leave this class.

LATIHAN 6

Your Indonesian penfriend is coming to Australia. In Indonesian, give five points of advice (**nasehat**) to your friend about things that he or she should bring or do before departure. Copy and complete the following table, beginning each piece of advice with **sebaiknya**.

Nasehat 1: Sebaiknya
Nasehat 2: Sebaiknya
Nasehat 3: Sebaiknya
Nasehat 4: Sebaiknya
Nasehat 5: Sebaiknya

28.6 How to say 'do not'

- **jangan**
- **dilarang**
- **tidak usah/tidak perlu**

Often we wish to tell people not to do something. The forms that we use to do this are called negative imperatives. In Indonesian, we have a choice of **jangan**, **dilarang** and **tidak usah**.

Jangan

This word simply means 'do not' and is neutral in terms of politeness and formality. Depending on how formal or urgent we want our sentence to be, we can also add **tolong**, **ya** and **dong**. As with the other uses, **tolong** makes a polite prohibition, whereas **ya** and **dong** create a sense of informality.

Note

When we use **jangan**, we can either keep or drop the **meN-** prefix.

> **Jangan (mem)baca sambil makan.**
> Don't read while eating.
>
> **Jangan (mem)baca sambil makan ya.**
> Don't read while eating, will you?
>
> **Jangan (mem)baca sambil makan dong.**
> Don't read while eating, will you?
>
> **Tolong jangan (mem)baca sambil makan.**
> Please don't read while eating.

Jangan can be also used alongside **mohon**, **harap**, **tolong**, **coba**, **ayo**, **hendaknya** and **sebaiknya**.

> **Harap jangan berdiri.** (formal, impersonal command)
> Please do not stand up.
>
> **Mohon jangan bicara keras-keras.** (formal, impersonal command)
> Please don't speak too loudly.
>
> **Tolong jangan panggil polisi.** (polite request)
> Please don't call the police.
>
> **Coba jangan menangis begitu.** (informal urging)
> Come on, don't cry like that.
>
> **Ayo jangan mencontoh pekerjaan temanmu.** (informal urging)
> Come on, don't copy your friend's work.
>
> **Sebaiknya jangan keluar kelas.** (polite advice)
> You had better not leave the class.

LATIHAN 7

Here is a cartoon strip from *Kisah Petualangan Tintin 'Bintang Jatuh'*. The third picture contains negative imperatives with **jangan**. Find out the meaning of the negative imperatives.

Dilarang

Literally meaning 'it is prohibited', this word is the passive form of the verb **melarang** (to prohibit) and is used primarily for public notices (official prohibitions). For instance, the following notice may be found at a spot where pedlars are not supposed to have their base of operations.

> **Dilarang berjualan di sini.**
> Do not do any selling here.

Other common notices are:

> **Dilarang membuang sampah di sini.**
> Do not throw rubbish here.

> **Dilarang masuk.**
> Do not enter.

Imperatives using **dilarang** are impersonal, formal and mostly used in written Indonesian. The person doing the prohibiting is not stated, but can be assumed. Because of this impersonal nature, we would not use this form in casual speech except in jest; for example, to tell a friend not to come to our house, or to tell your older sister not to be angry with you.

LATIHAN 8

Here is a picture showing a public sign with **dilarang**. What does the sign mean in English?

Tidak usah or tidak perlu

Both **tidak usah** (don't bother) and **tidak perlu** (there is no need) can be used for a wide variety of situations. Like **jangan**, these expressions are neutral in formality and politeness. However, **jangan** is more direct and, therefore, can be very appropriate if we want stronger prohibitions (for example, when we feel like being particularly harsh to someone).

As with **jangan**, the **meN-** prefix can be kept or dropped when we use **tidak usah** or **tidak perlu**.

> **Tidak perlu datang pagi-pagi sekali.**
> There is no need to come too early. (Don't come too early.)
>
> **Tidak usah (mem)beritahu ayahmu.**
> Don't bother to tell your father. (Don't tell your father.)
>
> **Tidak usah repot-repot bawa kado.**
> There is no need to bring a present. (Don't bother to bring a present.)

LATIHAN 9

Copy and complete the following table, giving five points of advice to your friends, who are about to go to Indonesia, on things that they should not do or that they do not need to do. Use **jangan**, **dilarang**, **tidak usah** or **tidak perlu**.

Example:

> Illegal drugs are prohibited, so you should not carry any.

There are lots of mosquitoes at night, so you should take some mosquito repellent.

Nasehat 1:
Nasehat 2:
Nasehat 3:
Nasehat 4:

LATIHAN 10

Below are some situations in which negative imperatives are appropriate. Write a sentence for each situation, using **jangan**, **dilarang**, **tidak usah** or **tidak perlu**.

1 You are inviting a friend to your birthday party. Tell him that he does not need to bring a present (**membawa**), but that he should not be late (**terlambat**).

2 Your little brother or sister keeps nagging you while you are studying. Tell him or her to stop bothering you (**mengganggu**).

3 You have been asked to put up a sign in class in Indonesian that prohibits people from using their mobile phones (**telepon genggam**) in class. What would you write? (**memakai**)

4 You have just failed your exam and feel terrible about it. Your teacher is telling you not to be discouraged. What would he or she say? (**berkecil hati**)

5 Your friend is new to town. You want to advise her not to go out at night by herself. What would you say? (**keluar**)

28.7 Imperatives in object-focus

Imperatives that are expressed as transitive sentences often appear in the object-focus (passive).

Object-focus imperatives are usually considered more polite, non-offensive and less direct than their corresponding subject-focus (active) imperatives, because the focus of our attention is shifted from the doer of the action (which, in most cases, is the person to whom we are speaking) to the object of the sentence. It is like saying 'Let this be done', rather than 'You do this'. This form of imperative is also very common in Indonesian, but often cannot be translated literally into English.

We can use object-focus imperatives for a wide variety of situations and with anybody. In fact, if you are not sure about whether or not you are being polite enough when you use the forms we have discussed so far, it is probably best to resort to the object-focus forms.

Object-focus imperatives are not the easiest forms to learn, but they represent a more natural way of saying 'Do this' in Indonesian.

Transforming subject-focus imperatives into object-focus imperatives

The rules for transforming subject-focus imperatives into object-focus imperatives are the same as those discussed in Chapter 19. The only differences are that, in subject-focus imperatives:

- there are imperative word(s) in the sentence
- the main verb has no prefix

Note

Only imperatives that use transitive verb(s) can be transformed into object-focus imperatives. (If there is no object, as in intransitive imperatives, there is nothing to be transformed.)

To make an object-focus imperative, follow these steps.

- Shift the object to the subject position or to a position following the imperative word(s), if there is no subject.
- Follow the object-focus rules for changing the verb form for first, second or third person.
- Keep the imperative word(s) and other words, such as adverb and prepositional phrase, where they are.

Prohibition:

Jangan	**beritahu**	**ayahmu.** (Subject-focus)
Negative imperative	*Verb*	*Object*
Do not	tell	your father.

Jangan	**ayahmu**	**diberitahu.** (Object-focus)
Negative imperative	*Object*	***di-*** *verb*

Literally: Don't let your father be told.
→ Don't let your father know.

Request:

Tolong ya	**temani**	**bapak**	**ke toko.** (Subject-Focus)
Imperative	*Verb*	*Object*	*Prepositional phrase*

Please accompany father to the shop, won't you?

Tolong ya	**bapak**	**ditemani**	**ke toko.** (Object-Focus)
Imperative	*Object*	***di-*** *verb*	*Prepositional phrase*

Literally: Please father be accompanied to the shop.
→ Please accompany father to the shop, won't you?

LATIHAN 11

Transform the following subject-focus imperatives into object-focus imperatives. The meaning of each object-focus imperative is provided. Remember that you have to follow the rules for first, second and third person subject for object-focus rules (refer to Chapter 19).

1 Urging (no subject)

IMPERATIVE	VERB	OBJECT	ADVERB
Ayo	habiskan	makannya	dulu

Literally: Come on, let the food be eaten first.
→ Come on, eat your food first.

2 Offering

IMPERATIVE	SUBJECT	VERB	OBJECT
Mari	saya	bawakan	kopernya

Literally: Here, the suitcase be carried by me for you.
→ Here, let me carry the suitcase for you.

3 Advising

IMPERATIVE	SUBJECT	VERB	OBJECT	ADVERB
Sebaiknya	kau	tanya	ibumu	dulu

Literally: It's better that your mother is asked by you first.
→ It's better that you ask your mother first. (You had better ask your mother first.)

LATIHAN 12

To further test how well you can shift your focus from the doer of the action to the object of that action, convert the following subject-focus imperatives into object-focus imperatives. Then translate each sentence into English.

1 Parent to a young child:
- **a** Ayo, pakai bajunya dulu.
- **b** Pakai dong sepatunya.
- **c** Ayo, minum susunya.

2 An employee to his or her boss:
- **a** Biar saya angkat barangnya.
- **b** Maaf Bu, minta tolong tandatangani cek ini.

3 To your close friend:
- **a** Tolong dong pinjami saya uang.
- **b** Antarkan saya ke dokter besok ya.

4 A teacher to his/her students:
- **a** Baca bab 6 untuk minggu depan.
- **b** Bantu temanmu yang baru itu.
- **c** Ketik tugas itu.

LATIHAN 13

Here is an interesting small rubric from the Indonesian newspaper *Kompas*. Find out what it is about. You may need to consult your dictionary for this exercise.

Yohanes Surya, Ph.D.

FISIKA itu ASYIK

Ambil UANG LOGAM, susun seperti gambar.
Letakkan GELAS berisi air di atasnya dan PIRING di atas gelas tersebut.

Lihat ke arah uang di bawah gelas, uang lenyap!

MENGAPA?

Masukkan TELUR dalam TOPLES berisi air garam.
Telur akan terapung (gambar a).
Tuang air tawar ke dalam toples itu hingga penuh (gambar b).
Ternyata telur berada di tengah.

Jawab:

- Menurut fisika, orang bisa melihat benda karena ada sinar datang dari benda ke mata. Sinar dan uang logam dibiaskan air. Sinar bias ini terhalang oieh piring hingga tidak sampai di mata. Itu sebabnya mata tidak dapat melihat uang tersebut.
- Menurut fisika, benda dengan massa jenis lebih besar akan tenggelam. Massa jenis telur lebih besar dari massa jenis air tawar tetapi lebih kecil dari massa jenis air garam. Itu sebabnya telur tenggelam di air tawar tetapi terapung di air garam.

Summary

- Imperatives: commands, requests, offering, inviting, urging, advising
- Negative imperatives: 'Do not'
- For intransitive verbs: no change to the verb
- For transitive verbs: drop the **meN-** prefix if the object is specific; retain if not
- Commands:
  —Informal: **ya**, **ayo**, **coba**, **dong**
  —Formal: **-lah**, **harap**, **mohon**, **hendaklah/nya**
- Requests: **minta**
  —Informal: **minta ya**, **minta dong**
  —Polite: **tolong (ya/dong)**, **minta tolong (ya/dong)**
  —Formal: **sudilah (kiranya)**
- Inviting: **mari**, **ayo**, **yuk**, **silakan**
- Offering: **ayo**, **mari**, **biar**, **silakan**
- Advising: **sebaiknya**
- Negative imperatives: **jangan**, **dilarang**, **tidak usah** or **tidak perlu**

29 Reporting What Has Been Said

Often we like to tell other people what someone has said or repeat what we ourselves have said. We do this either by quoting what has been said directly (*direct speech*) or indirectly (*indirect speech*); for example, using 'he/she/we/I/you/they said …'. In writing, direct speech is indicated by quotation marks.

Direct reporting:

> He said: 'The police came to our house last night.'
> I said to her: 'I forgot to return the library books.'

Indirect reporting:

> He said that the police came to their house last night.
> I said to her that I had forgotten to return the library books.

In this chapter we will learn how to report directly and indirectly in Indonesian.

29.1 'Say' verbs in Indonesian

To report directly in Indonesian, we can use the following words.

- **berkata/mengatakan** (to say)
- **bertanya** (to ask a question)
- **berujar** (to say, to comment)
- **bilang** (to say) (informal)
- **menambah** (to add)

29.2 Direct reporting

There are two ways to report or quote directly in Indonesian: one is by putting the 'he/she/we/I/you/they said …' part in front; the other is by putting it after we quote what was said.

If we put the 'he/she/we/I/you/they said …' part first, the prefix **ber-** or **me-** is retained (except for the verb **bilang**, which does not have a prefix).

> **Kakak saya berkata: 'Besok saya akan ke planetarium.'**
> My older sibling said: 'Tomorrow I will go to the planetarium.'
>
> **Mereka bertanya: 'Kapan hari ulang tahunmu?'**
> They asked: 'When is your birthday?'

If we quote first, the prefix is dropped and the subject (the person whose words you quote) comes after the verb.

> **'Besok saya akan ke planetarium,' kata kakak saya.**
> 'Tomorrow I will go to the planetarium,' my older sibling said.
>
> **'Kapan hari ulang tahunmu?' tanya mereka.**
> 'When is your birthday?' they asked.

If the subject is **dia**, it becomes **-nya** when the quote is mentioned first.

> **Dia bertanya: 'Kapan hari ulang tahunmu?'**
> He/she asked: 'When is your birthday?'
>
> **'Kapan hari ulang tahunmu?' tanyanya.**
> 'When is your birthday?' she asked.

Note

Bilang is an exception. Unlike the other words, its form does not change, whether you put it before or after the quote. It always follows the subject and it is never prefixed.

> **Dia bilang: 'Saya melihat hantu tadi malam.'**
> He/she said: 'I saw a ghost last night.'
>
> **'Saya melihat hantu tadi malam,' dia bilang.**
> 'I saw a ghost last night,' he/she said.

Remember that this verb is informal and is therefore more suitable for casual conversation or for e-mailing friends.

LATIHAN 1

Copy and complete the following, filling in the direct quote part of each sentence. Remember to put in the quotation marks.

KOSAKATA

mahasiswa university students
orang gila mad person

1	Orang gila itu bilang:	
2	Teman saya menambah:	
3	Orang itu berujar:	
4	Dokter Ratna berkata:	
5	Para mahasiswa bertanya:	
6		kata penjual buah-buahan itu.
7		ujar sopir truk itu.
8		bapak saya bilang.
9		tanyanya.
10		tambah mereka.

29.3 Indirect reporting

There are different ways to report indirectly, depending on what kind of sentence we are reporting.

Using *bahwa* for statements

If the sentence that we are reporting is a statement, we use **bahwa** (that) after the 'say' verb.

> **Dia berkata/mengatakan bahwa dia beragama Islam.**
> He/she said that he/she is a Muslim.

> **Anak kecil itu berkata/mengatakan bahwa dia suka sekali makan permen.**
> That child said that he/she really likes eating lollies.

Using *apakah* for 'yes' or 'no' questions

If what we are reporting is a question requiring a 'yes' or 'no' answer, we use **apakah** (if, whether), after the verb **bertanya** (to ask a question).

> **Indri bertanya apakah saya pernah melihat hantu.**
> Indri asked if I had ever seen a ghost.

> **Saya bertanya kepada kamu apakah mau ikut dan kamu bilang tidak.**
> I asked you whether you wanted to come along and you said you didn't.

LATIHAN 2

Report what the animals and people in the following pictures say using either **bahwa** (for statements) or **apakah** (for 'yes' or 'no' questions).

Reporting a 'wh-' question

- **apa** (what)
- **siapa** (who)
- **berapa** (how many/how much)
- **mengapa** (why)
- **bagaimana** (how)
- **yang mana** (which one)

If what we are reporting is a 'wh-' question (see Chapter 1), such as those listed above, we do not need to add anything after the verb **bertanya**, as shown in the following pictures.

Reporting a command

To report a command, we can use the following verbs and add **supaya** or **agar** after them.

- **menyuruh** (to tell someone to do something) + **supaya** (to)
- **meminta** (to ask to do something, to request) + **supaya** (to)

Sopir bis berkata: 'Jangan merokok di dalam bis ini!'
The bus driver said: 'Don't smoke on this bus!'

Sopir bis <u>menyuruh</u> penumpang <u>supaya</u> jangan merokok di dalam bis itu.
The driver told the passengers not <u>to</u> smoke on that bus.

Guru berkata kepada murid-murid: 'Kumpulkan tugas itu besok.'
The teacher said to the students: 'Submit the work tomorrow.'

Guru <u>menyuruh</u> murid-murid <u>supaya</u> mengumpulkan tugas itu besok.
The teacher told the students <u>to</u> submit the work tomorrow.

If the prefix of the verb in the command has been dropped (see Chapter 28), put it back.

Rini berkata: 'Bantu saya ya.'
Rini said: 'Help me, won't you?'

Rini <u>meminta</u> saya <u>supaya</u> <u>mem</u>bantu dia.
Rini asked me <u>to</u> help her.

Bapak berkata kepada saya: 'Tolong buang sampah ini.'
Father said to me: 'Please throw this rubbish away.'

Bapak <u>meminta</u> saya <u>supaya</u> <u>mem</u>buang sampah itu.
Father asked me <u>to</u> throw that rubbish away.

LATIHAN 3

Look at the following sets of pictures. Picture A has a command in direct speech. Write a sentence for Picture B using indirect speech, reporting what is said in Picture A.

1 Picture A

Picture B

2 Picture A

Picture B

Summary

- 'Say' verbs: **berkata/mengatakan**, **bertanya**, **berujar**, **bilang**, **menambah**
- Direct reporting:
  —Subject + 'say' verb (with prefix): '...'
  —'...', 'say' verb (no prefix) + subject
  —Exception: **bilang** (no change) → informal
- Indirect reporting:
  —Use **bahwa** ('that') for statements, **apakah** ('if, whether') for 'yes' or 'no' questions.
  —There is no need to add anything for 'wh-' questions.
  —Use **menyuruh/meminta** + **supaya** for commands.

30 Glossary

The following are the grammatical terms used in this book. The definition of each term is already given in the relevant chapters; however, this list may be useful as a quick reference.

abstract noun A noun that refers to something we cannot see or touch (e.g. **perasaan** 'emotion, feeling').

adjective A word that describes the quality of people (e.g. **cantik** 'beautiful'), things (e.g. bagus 'nice, good'), or places (e.g. **jauh** 'far').

adverb A word that indicates such things as frequency (e.g. **lima kali** 'five times'), manner (e.g. **pelan-pelan** 'slowly'), or time (e.g. **pagi ini** 'this morning').

affix A term used to refer to an incomplete word that is attached to the front or end of a base word.

agent A person (or another animate being) who is the instigator of an action.

aspect A word that shows whether an action is in process, completed or not yet completed (e.g. **sedang** 'in process of', **sudah** 'already', **belum** 'not yet').

auxiliary verb A word that expresses such things as aspect or modality and usually occurs before the main verb.

benefactive sentence A sentence construction involving a transitive verb that indicates that the action is done for the benefit of someone else. In Indonesian, the verb is usually suffixed by **-kan**.

beneficiary A person (or other animate being) who benefits from the action indicated by the verb.

causative sentence A sentence construction involving a transitive verb that indicates that the action 'causes' something to become what is indicated by the base word. In Indonesian, the verb has the suffix **-kan** (e.g. **membersihkan** 'to cause something to become clean, to clean') or -i (e.g. **mengotori** 'to cause something to become dirty').

circumfix A combination of a prefix and suffix, both attached to the same base word (e.g. **meN–kan in membesarkan**).

classifier A word whose function is to classify nouns according to shape or size (e.g. **ekor** 'tail' in **seekor anjing** 'a dog').

conditional sentence A sentence construction expressing a hypothesis or condition; an 'if' sentence.

conjunction A word that joins or links one part of a sentence to another.

demonstrative A pointing word (e.g. **ini** 'this', **itu** 'that').

direct speech A sentence used to tell other people what someone has said using the actual words uttered by that person.

ditransitive sentence A sentence construction involving a transitive verb that is followed by two objects, the first being the primary object and the second, the secondary object.

head The main word in a phrase. In a noun phrase (e.g. **kamar mandi** 'bathroom') the noun (**kamar**) is the head, while in a prepositional phrase (e.g. **di rumah** 'at home') the preposition (**di**) is the head.

imperative The sentence construction used to tell someone to do something. Imperative sentences range from commands and requests to invitations and offers.

indirect speech A sentence used to report what someone has said using our own words (i.e. not merely quoting).

interrogative sentence A sentence that expresses a question.

intransitive verb A verb that does not take an object (e.g. **lari** 'run', **tidur** 'sleep').

modality A word that expresses such concepts as possibility (e.g. **barangkali** 'maybe'), necessity (e.g. **harus** 'must') or ability (e.g. **bisa** 'can').

negative imperative An imperative form used to tell people not to do something (prohibition).

noun A word referring to either a person or a thing. When the thing cannot be seen or touched, the noun is called an 'abstract noun'.

noun phrase A group of words in which the noun is the main (head) word (e.g. **kamar tidur** 'bedroom').

object A noun or noun phrase that occurs directly after a transitive verb in a subject-focus (active) sentence. If the object refers to an entity affected by the action, it is called 'patient'; if it refers to an entity that benefits from the action, it is called 'beneficiary' or 'recipient'.

object-focus sentence A sentence construction in which the patient/beneficiary/recipient of the action is mentioned first because it is the focus of our attention.

patient An entity (person or thing) that is the object of a transitive verb and is affected by the action of the verb (e.g. **dia** in **saya memukul dia**).

phrase A group of words that function like a noun. A phrase in which the main word is a noun is called a noun phrase.

prefix An affix that is put before a base word.

preposition A word that occurs before a noun, noun phrase or pronoun to indicate a location or time (e.g. **di**, **pada**, **kepada**).

prepositional phrase A phrase that typically consists of a preposition followed by a noun or temporal phrase (e.g. **di rumah** 'at home', **pada jam 5** 'at 5 o'clock').

primary object The object that directly follows the verb in a ditransitive construction.

pronoun A word that can substitute for a noun referring to an entity that is known (e.g. **saya** 'I', **mereka** 'they').

reciprocal verb A verb that indicates a mutual action or relationship between two people or objects (e.g. **berpandangan** 'look at each other').

secondary object An object that follows the primary object in a ditransitive sentence.

stative verb A verb that describes a state rather than an action (e.g. **terbalik** 'upside down, back to front').

subject A noun or noun phrase that generally goes before the verb and refers to the 'doer' of an action.

subject-focus sentence A sentence in which the subject gets the focus of our attention and is mentioned first before the verb.

suffix An affix that is attached to the end of a base word.

tag A word that is like a question word and is added at the end of a statement, either to ask a question or to tell someone about something (e.g. **bukan** in **Itu Hasan, bukan**? 'That's Hasan, isn't it?').

topic–comment sentence A sentence in which there is a topic (something the sentence is focused on) commented upon in the rest of the sentence.

transitive verb A verb that takes an object and this object directly follows it (e.g. **membeli** 'buy'). Some verbs can have both a transitive and intransitive use (e.g. **makan** 'eat').

verb A word that refers to an action (e.g. **makan** 'to eat') or state (e.g. **tertutup** 'shut').

31

Index